ENDORSEMENTS

Steve Stewart's new book, *The Journey*, is a heart touching book that reveals the love, mercy, and empowering grace of God. Written by a man whose heart is touched by the poor and marginalized, who has given much of his life in showing mercy to them, and has been able to do so because God has given Steve His enabling grace. I have been with Steve in the nations and worked with him to lift up the poor and forgotten. I highly recommend both *The Journey* and Steve Stewart to the reading audience.

Randy Clark
Founder of Global Awakening,
The Apostolic Network of Global Awakening,
author, and creator of The Christian Healing Certification
Program and The Christian Prophetic Certification Program

Powerful stories of God-encounters among the great saints are inspiring, but can also be disempowering for regular folks. In *The Journey*, Steve Stewart breaks that mold with testimonies that echo the book of Acts. Yet these kingdom works break out, not through mighty apostles, but through the hands and hearts of humble servants and spiritual rookies. Truly, blessed are the poor in spirit; theirs is the kingdom of heaven!

Brad Jersak
Editor-in-chief, CWR magazine
Faculty (NT and Patristics), Westminster Theological Centre

Steve Stewart, in his book *The Journey* shares the amazing way God is using Impact Nations to advance the Kingdom. Caring and providing for the poor, offering medical care to those who normally wouldn't have it, and praying for the sick with miraculous results are all a normal part of these *Journeys of Compassion*. Steve shares how so often God has gone before them and opened amazing doors for the team.

If you are in need of encouragement in your walk with the Lord, read a few chapters of this book and you be put in touch with the goodness and mercy of our Lord. I highly recommend it!

Joe McIntyre
Founder and Senior Minister,
Word of His Grace Church and Empowering Grace Ministries
President, Kenyon's Gospel Publishing Society

Steve Stewart has faith and as you read these testimonies you will too. With compelling ardor Steve opens windows into the world of the supernatural love of God. Best of all, he does it in a way that makes you know that you too can experience firsthand what it means to live in the power of God. What a privilege to endorse Steve and his ever-expanding witness to the glory of God here and now. Danger! Reading may make you lie awake at night and it will definitely change you.

Alan Hawkins
Founder, New Life City

The power of the gospel to transform individual lives has been clearly evident in Jesus and His followers. Steve Stewart is echoing the call that comes from the very heart of a loving God. There is enough power and love in this book to transform entire societies! Receive it!

Leif Hetland
President- Global Mission Awareness
Author- 'Seeing Through Heaven's Eyes'

THE JOURNEY

35 STORIES OF KINGDOM ENCOUNTERS

STEVE STEWART

THE JOURNEY:
35 STORIES OF KINGDOM ENCOUNTERS

Published By Impact Nations
Copyright © 2015 by Steve Stewart

ISBN: 1517210925

Impact Nations
3620 Wyoming Blvd NE Suite 222
Albuquerque NM 87111
Phone: 1-877-736-0803
Email: info@impactnations.com

TABLE OF CONTENTS

FOREWORD
JOHN ARNOTT

I have always been enthralled with Holy Ghost stories. I was amazed by the testimonies of healing from Kathryn Kuhlman's meetings. I was inspired by the miracles that happened in John Wimber's conferences. Since the time of being a new Christian, I have been encouraged and influenced by revival accounts of our Christian legacy throughout all of church history, from the book of Acts to present day.

Recently, in Lyon France, I was reminded of the account of Blondin, a 15 year old girl from the second century who was tortured and burned to death by the Romans for her unwavering faith in Jesus Christ. Her witness of faithfulness continues to this very day. People who have been powerfully touched by God will inevitably have an amazing story to tell, often with great cost and sacrifice. Carol and I have our own powerful stories that have changed us forever. It is our continual joy and delight to hear the unending accounts of transformed lives through the ongoing Toronto revival that we still enjoy this very day.

Christianity and Revival however have always been driven by the stories of people who have been miraculously touched by God. The Bible also contains a great many personal testimonies of how the lives of ordinary people were transformed forever by the touch of God.

This book, *The Journey*, contains many of these Holy Ghost stories and God encounters, as seen and told through the lives and ministry of Steve and Christina Stewart. We have known each other for almost 30 years and both of us as couples have been heavily involved in church planting, in global missions, and in revival both at home and abroad. For the last 10 years or so, Steve and Christina have focused on global mission work - food for the hungry, fresh clean water, relief work with various international disasters - all with a compassionate emphasis on needy women and children. This book encompasses the story of their ministry, Impact Nations. It is a story of the transformation of the lives of many people who have joined their teams to travel with them. It also includes the miraculous stories of thousands that they and their mission teams have ministered to.

One of my favorite accounts is of Mike, a street kid out on his own in Nakuru, Kenya since he was orphaned at eight years old. He was a thief and a pickpocket, doing anything necessary to stay alive one more day. He was a survivor! He used to love going to evangelistic crusades. His comment: "If you can't pick pockets while people are worshipping with their hands in the air, then you can't pick pockets." But one day it backfired; he ended up listening to the message and surrendering his heart and life to Jesus Christ. I am sure there is a lot more to his discipleship journey, but today he is active in ministry especially with the poor, helping people from similar backgrounds to his own. In this book, Steve recounts how Mike is extremely burdened for imprisoned women in Kenya. They are heavily fined for street vending without a permit and since they cannot pay for these permits, they are put in jail, along with their children for 6 months to a year. Impact Nations endeavors to raise the $80-90 needed to pay the fines of these women and then help train them and set them up with a micro business to break this devilish cycle of poverty. Mike continues to find more and more of these people who need help and Steve and Christina do their best to see them set free with a fresh start as the gospel is shared and the testimony of watching Jesus making a way for them unfolds in front of them.

It is difficult to fully recount the long-term impact of the ministry of Impact Nations. Scores of countries, hundreds of different and challenging situations, and many thousands of lives transformed. The needy are being fed and clothed but so much more than that is happening. They are becoming followers of Jesus, are growing in the Word of God and are encountering the Holy Spirit, which is life changing for them and many nations are impacted for the Kingdom of God.

The Journey is just Part 1 of their story. Part 2 and 3 are still before us in disasters that have not yet happened, the horrendous needs of people that we have not yet met or perhaps are not yet even born. Jesus said that the poor are always with us (Matt 26:11) yet we are all admonished by the Lord to minister to the poor and bring the Kingdom of Love, Healing and Redemption to them. This is where the Holy Spirit excels. He delights to use the likes of Steve and Christina Stewart to make a global difference and to bring

God's Heavenly Kingdom to earth, but He also loves to see straight into the hearts and lives of desperate, needy, precious souls for whom Jesus died.

These thrilling real life stories will take you into the personal struggles and victories of real-life people who have experienced a Holy Spirit breakthrough. You will be thrilled by the miracle healings: the blind see, the deaf hear, the dead are raised, and the poor have the Gospel opened up to them.

The Kingdom of God is making a huge difference all over the world. There is a lot of tragedy and disaster going on globally and yet God is moving powerfully and relentlessly in every nation. We are in a mighty wave of revival, and have not seen the likes of it since the days of the early church. I want to invite you, with Steve and Christina Stewart, to join in and become part of the only solution that works to change the world.

What can I do you ask? Support them with your prayers and finances, but even more than that, prayerfully consider going on an outreach with Impact Nations (www.impactnations.org). It is here that God will supernaturally provide funds and direction. You will go with an amazing team of new friends who are nervous just like you are. You will witness many Holy Spirit encounters at a level that your eyes have not seen before and perhaps best of all, God will use 'little old you' to do miracles through your words and hands. I have so often been amazed at the win-win blessing that happens when Western Christians go on short-term missions to the developing world. The people we go to serve and help have their hope restored and their lives revolutionized by the miracles and power of God but in turn you and I come home transformed as well as we realize that miracles are for today, and God wants to release them through you!!! You will return home with renewed faith and fervor to see salvation and healing continue in your community.

So enjoy this book. Enter into the stories, laugh and cry along with the people who have already received their miracle. Allow their testimonies to inspire you to receive your own miracle and may you go and play your part in changing the world.

So read on, dear reader, read on, and may the Holy Spirit fall wonderfully upon you as you do.

John Arnott
Catch The Fire, Toronto

PREFACE

I pray also that the eyes of your heart may be enlightened
in order that you may know the hope to which he has called
you, the riches of his glorious inheritance in the saints.

EPHESIANS 1:18

One of my greatest pleasures is to watch men and women awaken to new possibilities in their lives and in the world around them, to discover the sheer joy of living in step with the rhythm of God. These stories from the past three decades have been written with the hope that they will encourage followers of Jesus who carry deeply in their hearts a hope for something *more*. They are my stories; they are my friends' stories; they are the stories of some of the hundreds of people who have travelled with me to remote villages around the developing world. The Apostle Paul told us that the purpose of prophecy is to encourage, strengthen and comfort. By those criteria, I hope that these stories are prophetic. They are filled with testimonies of God's miraculous intervention. Very often, the testimony of the breaking by God into one person's life will somehow release a miracle in the life of the listener. May it be so with these stories.

This collection is set in North America and overseas, especially among poor communities in Africa, Asia, and Central America. The settings reflect my years as a pastor in Canada; my work in Russia, which began after the fall of the Soviet Union; and especially my years directing Impact Nations, an organization that works with partners in the developing world to proclaim and demonstrate God's Kingdom in supernatural and practical ways.

The seed for Impact Nations was planted twelve years ago on a flight back from ministering in Korea. On that flight, the Lord surprised me with a question: "What do you want to do with the rest of your life? I'll let you do anything." A short time later, I answered, "If I can really do anything with the rest of my life, then I want to rescue lives. I want to rescue them spiritually, economically, medically, educationally and socially." Although no one knew (except my wife) what had happened on that plane, within two weeks I started receiving invitations to come to various places where I had never traveled before. Over time, more people began to travel with me and Impact Nations was born.

The Journey is intended to be more than a collection of stories about miracles—although remembering and recording those has been a delightful experience. Many of the stories are invitations to ponder the amazing breadth and power of the Gospel; others shine a light on the invisible ones, those people who are all too easily forgotten. In writing these stories, an overarching theme gradually emerged: God is continually moving, reconciling all of creation to Himself in Christ; and where He moves, His way is marked by rescue and restoration. This is the God-dance. This is what we were made for.

Stephen Stewart

1

WHERE THE LIGHT SHINES

One day, while many were abandoning Him, Jesus turned to his friends and asked, "Are you going to leave too?" Peter answered for them all when he said, "Where else could we go, Lord? You alone have the words of eternal life." Peter had gone too far, had seen and heard too much, his heart was too captured to ever turn back. He was hooked, and he knew it.

I remember when I was hooked. It happened as I stood among 1,200 nearly starving students in St. Petersburg, Russia during the first week of January, 1992.

Six months earlier I had been driving my family home from our yearly vacation. Without notice, when I wasn't thinking of anything in particular, the Lord spoke to me and said, "Go to the Soviet Union." After pondering this thought for a moment, I replied, "Where in the Soviet Union? It's a big country." "Leningrad" was all He said. (Shortly thereafter the city returned to its historic name, St. Petersburg.) End of conversation—but it stayed with me day after day for weeks. I didn't know what to do about it, so I just pondered on this strange message. Then on August 19, 1991, the unthinkable

1

happened. More rapidly than anyone could have imagined, the Communist Party lost its iron grip on the nation. Gorbachev was captured, then released in a failed military coup. When the soldiers refused to shoot their own citizens, the coup was over, but the floodgates had suddenly opened to profound (albeit, chaotic) social change—and with it, economic and political collapse.

All this time, I was feeling like I had failed by not actively responding to the word God had given me; it seemed that I had missed my opportunity. Then, in October, God initiated unexpected invitations and connections that thrust me forward into the midst of historic events. Although I had never before been on a mission trip, on December 30, 1991 I flew with a small team into Russia during the very week that the Soviet Union was dissolved. I had grown up in the 1950's and 60's at a time when we were taught to fear the Soviet Union as the evil empire that was determined to take over the world. I was surprised how tense I felt when I found myself standing alone on the airport tarmac at 2 am, accompanied by three armed Russian soldiers. Minutes later, I was reunited with our team, but the impression of that moment still remains with me.

In the midst of the economic, social and political chaos of the Soviet Union's sudden collapse, St. Petersburg assaulted the senses with an almost unbelievable mix of grandeur and desperation. This historic city with over 100 palaces, gold-domed cathedrals and ornate state buildings was now filled with beggars and those who continued to go to work every day—but who hadn't been paid in months. I remember the old people lining up for hours in order to buy a single loaf of bread for their family. And I recall my amazement when the deputy mayor of the city told me that for years the Soviet Union had been like a movie façade, looking impressive from the front, but with no substance behind it. Now the façade had fallen down.

In a country ruled by fear for so many decades, people could not now suddenly begin to trust each other and work together. Too often openness had led to betrayal in the past. The oppression and suspicion were palpable. (Our hotel rooms were bugged, something very unnerving for us from the West. Russians who visited my room would immediately gesture for silence, choosing to communicate through written notes.)

And yet, as is so often the case around the world, the light of the Gospel shines in the midst of such darkness. Our team distributed illustrated booklets about Jesus, His life and message. We passed out many thousands of them on the streets and in the vast subway system that transported three million people a day. And everywhere the response was remarkable: men and women began to weep; others would quickly crowd around us; I was kissed on the face, the hands, the neck. For 74 years, it had been illegal to share the Gospel, or even to own a Bible. But now, the floodgates had opened.

My wife and two other ladies began to hand out Bibles in the foyer of a theatre. Immediately a crowd gathered, then seemed to grow exponentially. Four policemen saw what was happening from the street and ran in to form a human wall between the ladies and the crowd, afraid that they would be crushed.

Occasionally we experience events that, upon reflection, we come to realize have marked us forever, perhaps even changing the direction of our lives. What happened over the next day was such an event for me.

Several weeks earlier, before going to Russia, the Lord had connected me with a man who had arranged for two buses filled with food and clothing to be driven into the city. He could not go himself, so he asked our team to oversee its distribution at a college dorm for young families. The buses were accompanied all the way from the Finnish border—120 miles away—by an entourage of police vehicles, with lights flashing and sirens blaring. The supplies were unloaded into a basement storage room in the dormitory and a 24-hour police guard was posted at the door.

Upon first seeing the dormitory, I was struck with how incredibly dilapidated it was. It looked like something from a novel by Charles Dickens—dirty and cold, with a pervasive odor of decay. The 1,200 people at this college had been surviving on extremely small rations for several months. After setting up in the gymnasium, we began to invite the young families in, about 100 people at a time. Packages of food had been set on tables from one end of the room to the other. Their reactions to this sight displayed a wide spectrum of emotions—laughter, shouting, stunned silence, tears. Etched in my mind is a picture of a young mother who, while holding her baby, sagged against a pillar and wept uncontrollably at the sight of the food set out on the tables. It took hours, but every family received enough food staples to last for several weeks. They also received warm clothes.

Even without preaching (that came the next day), there was a remarkable sense of the presence of Jesus in that room. I experienced what it was like to "Come and share your master's happiness" (Matthew 25:21). I had come to *give;* instead, at a deep, deep level, I had *received.* I had encountered Jesus and that encounter has marked and directed my life from that day to this.

Etched in my mind is a picture of a young mother who sagged against a pillar and wept uncontrollably at the sight of the food.

If we are looking for Jesus, we will always find Him among the hungry and thirsty, among the sick, the lonely and the imprisoned. Always, because as He already told us, that is where He is, waiting for us to come meet with Him.

2

I WILL TURN THEIR MOURNING INTO JOY

The dream began in my heart when I repeatedly encountered destitute women in the village of Kalonga, Uganda. They were either young widows or women abandoned by their husbands, desperately trying to keep their children from dying of starvation or disease. They were homeless or living in dreadful conditions, incredibly poor even by the impoverished standards of rural African villages. These women lived a kind of local nomadic life, constantly being driven from place to place. I don't know what impacted me more, the sight of their children with bloated stomachs and the orange hair that comes from severe malnutrition, or the expressions on the women's faces, reflecting the deep sadness and profound hopelessness that came from seeing no other possible future.

Jesus said that the Gospel is good news to the poor. This has to mean more than, one day, after a life of deprivation and suffering, they will finally go to heaven. The Gospel is meant to be good news *right now*.

Compelled by this conviction, but not really knowing

what to do, I simply started sharing the story of these women wherever I went. Meanwhile my son, Ben, flew over to Uganda and made a short film about the plight of the widows that we subsequently posted on the Impact Nations website. We then located some fertile land outside the village that was for sale. Before long, through the generosity of people in the West whose hearts had been impacted, we had the money necessary to purchase the land. And so the adventure began.

Three months later, I was back in Uganda, leading another team on a Journey of Compassion. I vividly recall my great excitement as we drove into Kalonga. There was much to see and do that day, but as soon as possible, I headed over to what the locals now called, "the widows' land". After a short ride and a bit of a hike, I came around a bend in the trail and there it was: rising up a long, gentle slope with a large tree at the top. Before me was the land I had dreamt about. In my mind, I had pictured green meadows just waiting to be tilled and turned into gardens and cornfields. What I actually saw stopped me in my tracks. There were large bushes and brambles everywhere. The ground looked rock hard. If this land had ever been cultivated, it had been a long, long time ago. I suddenly felt totally overwhelmed. The task was simply too big. How could these women ever turn this land into a good and fruitful place to live?

But the Lord never seems to leave us without hope. As I walked up the hill, my eyes were drawn to the sight of a woman beginning to clear a piece of land near the big tree at the top. As she cut into the ground again and again with a large mattock, I felt a flicker of confidence that this dream really would be fulfilled. There really would be a community of women and children, each with their own piece of land, each with their own crops and each with their own home that nobody would be able to take away. But still…the task seemed so overwhelming.

Twelve parcels of the widows' land were distributed by our partner in Kalonga—Pastor John, a wonderful shepherd who not only cares for the people in his congregation, but also cares for most of the townsfolk. He went to the most needy women (and a few refugee families who had escaped from the violence in the Congo), offering each of them a parcel of the land. With every visit, an entirely different future suddenly opened for the women and their children; they could hardly believe what they were hearing. But Pastor John told me something else that amazed me. On a few occasions, instead of receiving the gift of the land, a woman would tell Pastor John that she knew of a family even more needy than herself and so, would he mind giving the land to that family? In the midst of such desperate poverty, how is such generosity possible?

In the midst of such desperate poverty, how is such generosity possible?

•   •   •

Nine months later, I was back in Kalonga. Here is what I journaled:

"The land is now fully cultivated. The bushes and weeds are all gone. In their place are vegetable gardens, corn and bean fields, and seven simple homes. They have already had one harvest since receiving the land in March; they are now planting and cultivating for another. On the day we walked around the land there was a group of the community working together to build another mud house. First they build a framework, then pack it with mud. When it fully dries in a week, a final smooth coat of mud goes on. It is hard work, but what I heard was the sound of much laughter and joking. It was a delight to see them working together, helping one another to succeed."

We spoke with several widows and families about their new life. All were happy, but one stood out for me. Agnes is the mother of six. She told me that as good as it is to have fertile land, the greatest blessing is having her own home. She now enjoys a security that she had not known before. Now Agnes does not have to choose between homelessness and working all day on someone's land just to raise money for rent. Instead, when her crops are planted, she can work for someone else and keep the money she earns to improve her children's lives. She was so happy to tell us about how for the first time she and her family were starting to thrive. Agnes proudly showed me her new tin roof, which she had paid for by working for three farmers, helping to harvest their corn crop.

I cannot describe the joy and admiration that I feel. These families have created a safe, supportive community. They have done it through hard, hard work. They labor all day, every day (except Sundays, when they go to church to celebrate, worship and eat together). Whereas I looked at the land and felt overwhelmed, they only saw great opportunity.

Repeatedly, the women come and thank me for all I have done. Each time, I feel great embarrassment. It is I who thank them. After all, what did I do but raise awareness of their plight and ask for financial help from people who have more than enough? It is these women who are the heroes. *They* are the ones who, day after day, break up the ground, plant and tend the crops, take in the harvest, so that their children can have a future.

●   ●   ●

Seven months pass, and I am back in Kalonga.

Four months prior, we had purchased more land on the opposite side of the village for another 20 families. And now almost half of it has been cleared and crops are growing. Seven houses have been built. While our team is here, we help two more widows build their houses. I am thankful for what has happened on this land, but I look forward to getting over to the original widows' land to see how they have progressed.

On my last afternoon, I am finally able to visit the original land. It is about an hour before sunset and the late, golden light makes the Ugandan countryside breathtakingly beautiful. As I hike the same trail that I first took to the widows' land eighteen months ago, my heart is full. I can still remember so clearly how I felt that first time.

I have a few friends with me this time, and as we come to the land, we are greeted by a large group of small children. They are all shouting and laughing at once and, as always, they are touching our strange, white skin. Soon we are joined by a number of the women. I am hugged and kissed by many.

The land is beautiful. Everywhere, there are gardens and a wide variety of crops—sweet potatoes, cabbage, spinach, carrots and corn. They tell me about the beans that were recently harvested. One after another, the women pull me by the hand to show me their gardens and their homes. All of the homes are built now; many have metal roofs, some houses have two rooms. There is a remarkable pride of ownership. Everywhere is clean. They tell me about their plans for raising chickens. I even see a couple of pigs. And always I hear the sound of laughter. One after another the women tell me how happy they are. All of their children are now going to school. I see no bloated stomachs or orange hair. There are no sad faces here.

•   •   •

Beyond the beautiful transformation that has taken place on this land, there is something even more wonderful. This is a prophetic community that both points to, and reflects, God's great promise of a new creation. When I first saw that solitary woman breaking up the ground under the large tree, this prophetic pledge came to mind:

For I will create a new heaven and a new earth,
The past events will not be remembered nor come to
*   mind.*
Then be glad and rejoice forever in what I am
*   creating…*
People will build houses and live in them;
They will plant vineyards and eat their fruit.

They will not build and others live in them;
They will not plant and others eat.
For My people's lives will be like the lifetime of
    a tree.
My chosen ones will fully enjoy the work of
    their hands.
They will not labor without success or bear children
    destined for disaster,
For they will be a people blessed by the LORD along
    with their descendants. (Isaiah 65:17, 18, 21-23)

This is His great and cosmic promise: to not only restore, but to create something new, where the reality of heaven becomes our reality. To see, and then to take faltering steps toward what we see—this is where we discover His grace, His empowering presence like a wind at our backs, leading and giving us the power to move with Him in His dream of justice and restoration.

This is His great and cosmic promise: to not only restore, but to create something new, where the reality of heaven becomes our reality.

"Beauty for ashes; joy for sadness; praise for
    despair." (Isaiah 61:3)

Oh, what You have done Lord, what You have done.

3

INSIDE A JOURNEY OF COMPASSION: PART 1

For eleven years I have been taking people into the frontlines of ministry around the developing world, on what we call *Journeys of Compassion*. As of this writing, people have registered over 1,100 times for forty-five trips to fifteen nations. Journeys of Compassion put hands and feet to the adventure of the Gospel, where together we live out the reality that the Kingdom of God is big enough and powerful enough to touch every part of life. Everywhere we go, Christ is preached, the sick are healed, and good news to the poor is demonstrated through ministry in prisons, hospitals, mobile medical clinics and feeding programs.

Many of the stories in this book come from these Journeys. Again and again, I have heard men and women tell me how coming on a Journey has radically changed their perspective of the Gospel, the world and themselves. And so, to help you better understand how these stories have unfolded, here are some of my journal excerpts from one Journey of Compassion—to Kenya in 2013. I have taken teams to different parts of Kenya since 2005; on each trip we saw the Lord move powerfully—whether in remote mountain communities, in city slums, in the Muslim territory of Eastern Kenya, or even in Dadaab, the largest refugee camp in the world. However, perhaps more than any other, the 2013 Journey was filled with healing, miracles and supernatural surprises.

Enjoy.

KENYA 2013: DAY ONE JOURNAL ENTRY

This morning, the team gathered for orientation. Before beginning, Mike Brawan, (our partner in Kenya) spoke to us about the impact of last year's Journey. He brought several locals with him. We met a woman who had been imprisoned along with her children for years; last year we were able to pay her fine and she was freed. Now she has a job helping other women to integrate into society when they come out of prison. We met Fatima, a Muslim who last year heard the Gospel at one of our clinics and received the Lord. She now works daily with the Muslims who have become followers of Jesus. She also evangelizes in her Muslim community. As a result of last year's clinic and outreach, there is now a thriving church of Muslim followers of Jesus. On Thursday, *Impact Nations*

We met Fatima, a Muslim who last year heard the Gospel at one of our clinics and received the Lord. She now works daily with the Muslims who have become followers of Jesus.

is going back to do a medical clinic and outreach in this Muslim community.

Last year, a door opened for us to distribute 27,500 doses of anti-parasite medicine to the school children. This went on for weeks after the Journey ended (though we were able to distribute several thousand ourselves while we were there). Besides receiving the medicine, each student was offered prayer. Today, we met Simon, who as a direct result of the anti-parasite distribution, now oversees a team of young men and women who are discipling over *4,000* high school students *every week*. This has become the biggest youth fellowship in all of Kenya. The government is delighted with the results that Simon's team is getting; in fact, they have provided him with an office next to the office of the district governor.

Today, we met Simon, who as a direct result of the anti-parasite distribution, now oversees a team of young men and women who are discipling over 4,000 high school students every week.

Besides strengthening the young people in their walk with the Lord, Simon's team is helping them find employment after finishing school, including working as tutors in the 11 high schools in the city (providing them with even more opportunity to share the Gospel and disciple others). All of this started with Impact Nations going into the schools with medicine for the students. What the Lord has done is amazing.

One of the key members of the Kenyan parliament also

came to speak to us about the effect that last year's Journey had on the country. Her particular area of interest is women, especially the weakest and most vulnerable. After she spoke, we had an opportunity to pray for her. Several of the team had powerful prophetic words, which impacted this woman greatly.

Mike and his ministry (Metro Church) are being added to daily. Their work is primarily with the poor, the widow, the orphan, the prisoner and the outcast. As a result, they are faced with the challenge of how to care for all of these new believers, beyond praying for them and telling them to come to church. They have met this challenge by incorporating the new believers into small house churches, where they experience the healing and care of being part of a family. As well, Mike provides small loans (not gifts) and trains them to start businesses of their own. They begin by working alongside another who is further down the road. After they learn the basics of the business first-hand, they are given a loan and helped to start their own business. So far, Mike and his team have seen *1,200* businesses started and operating!

As I heard the reports of all that the Lord did out of the Journey last year, I kept thinking about John 15:16: *"You did not choose Me, but I chose you and appointed you that you might go and bear fruit—fruit that will last."*

What a privilege and joy.

DAY THREE JOURNAL ENTRY

Yesterday, the team conducted the first medical clinic of this Journey. It was held in Metro Church (Mike's church), but most of the people who came were from the neighborhood. Our medical people who had been to Nakuru last year, were struck by how much sicker the people were this time. Besides the 40 people who had teeth pulled by the dentist, about 225 other people were treated, but that isn't a very good reflection of the amount of medical care that happened. At 4 pm when the clinic was supposed to be closed, there were still over 55 people waiting to receive their medicine from the pharmacy. The pharmacy team worked until 6:30 filling and dispensing medicine. This was an indication of just how sick the people were with infections, malaria, dysentery, fevers and more.

Meanwhile, the prayer team saw wonderful things happen. From the very beginning until the end, God was healing the sick. During the opening prayer over the crowd that were waiting for the clinic, God sovereignly healed a child of a high fever. Once the team started laying hands on the sick and praying, things really took off. They saw someone with a totally blind eye receive sight; a woman completely deaf in one ear had her hearing fully restored. One woman who came could not walk. Her foot was very swollen and caused her too much pain to put any weight on it. While praying, the team member watched all the swelling go down in front of his eyes. The woman got up and walked normally—and with no pain. A man came in leaning on a cane; he left the clinic holding it in his hand! Cataracts disappeared, pain left, malaria fevers vanished. For some of the prayer team, this was the first time they had experienced anything like this.

The woman got up and walked normally—and with no pain. A man came in leaning on a cane; he left the clinic holding it in his hand!

At 5:30, we left the pharmacy team still working and drove to a slum region across town. It was near a market area, and the only place to preach was across the street (a narrow dirt lane) from where the people stood. It was very late by the time we started, so I only spoke for a few minutes. When the invitation was made to come to Jesus, over 60 people crossed the street and prayed. It was interesting that a high percentage were men who were taking this decision very seriously. The team gathered around those who came forward and prayed for infilling by the Holy Spirit. Following this, we prayed for the sick. As the team prayed, God healed. Several who had not come forward at the invitation, now gave their lives to Jesus.

As always, the Metro team did a great job of getting each new believer's contact information. Everyone will be followed up. I have never worked with a team that is so committed to discipling each one who comes to Jesus. And given how many healings and salvations we have seen in just three days, I wonder how much more fruit we will see in the coming days.

> "My Father is glorified by this: that you produce much fruit and prove to be My disciples." (John 15:8, 16)

4

INSIDE A JOURNEY OF COMPASSION: PART TWO

KENYA 2013: DAY FOUR JOURNAL ENTRY

The team made history today. For the first time ever, a medical clinic was held in Bondeni, the poorest area in Nakuru. It is a Muslim neighborhood, where the people live in terrible squalor. We were told to keep our backpacks on at all times—and not on our backs, but on our fronts so that no one could reach in without our knowing. These were the sickest people that we have encountered yet in Africa. The area was crowded, with the clinic spread out on either side of an open sewer. Yet, the people waited patiently and there was greater and greater peace as time went by. We were visited by local dignitaries, who came to make sure that we were alright. We were just fine. Then the president of Kenya television arrived all the way from Nairobi (about 3 hours away). Mike and I were interviewed by a newspaper, and two different television networks. I was asked by one reporter what the greatest need was in order to improve the health of the people. I answered that they need access to safe drinking water; with this, sickness, skin disease, infections etc. would immediately drop dramatically.

Once again, the team worked very well together; over 200 people received medical care. The prayer team was busy all day. Many Muslims were happy to receive prayer in the name of Jesus; many healings took place. By the end of the day, 48 people from the neighborhood had prayed to receive Jesus. This was a very big decision for each of them, as they knew that in doing so they would face rejection, criticism and perhaps even violence. All of these new believers will be discipled and cared for in the church that was started last year for Muslim believers. At the end of the day, many came to Mike and his team, expressing gratitude that a team had come and given care and love in such a practical and needed manner.

48 people from the neighborhood had prayed to receive Jesus. This was a very big decision for each of them, as they knew that in doing so they would face rejection, criticism and perhaps even violence.

Oh, and about our bags and other stuff being stolen. There was absolutely no problem all day. Then as we were leaving, we saw Mike give one of the boys some money to share with the others. It seems that Mike had gone to them at the beginning of the clinic and promised that if everything stayed peaceful and nothing went missing, that he would pay the boys!

It is always interesting working with Mike. As a man who himself grew up on the streets, he has a great influence (and wisdom) with the poorest street people in this city of over a million persons.

DAY FIVE JOURNAL ENTRY

Today, while the ladies attended the women's conference, Mike took four of the men out for what he calls "guerrilla evangelism". They went to a poor area of the city and parked the truck in the middle of a large empty field. After about 15 minutes of music being piped out from Mike's ministry truck, a large crowd gathered. Each of the men shared; some preached and some gave their testimony. At one point while Vinnie (from Australia) was giving his powerful testimony, people began to weep and some even fell to their knees. Vinnie joined them there and prayed for them. Mike then gave an invitation to receive Jesus and asked people to come over to have their names recorded so that they could be followed up. *447 people gave their names*. Our entire time in the field was only about 45 minutes. Wherever we turn in Kenya, we are overwhelmed with the readiness of men, women and children to receive Christ.

More feedback from Bondeni keeps coming in. It is the poor Muslim community where we did the clinic two days ago. The community is overwhelmed with thanksgiving for what happened. Any ideas they had that Christians hated Muslims or looked down on them (as the minority group in Kenya) were dispelled. We keep hearing more stories of men and women from Bondeni turning to Jesus. Mercy truly *does* triumph over judgment. If we will activate our faith, if we will *get moving* in the direction and rhythm of the King, He does amazing things: Thy Kingdom come, Lord.

If we will activate our faith, if we will get moving in the direction and rhythm of the King, He does amazing things.

We are all here to help people. Jesus said that all that God wants from us is to love Him and love people. Micah 6:8 tells us that God has already shown us exactly what He wants from all of us: act with justice, love mercy, stay humble.

I know of nothing more rewarding, more exciting, more fulfilling than simply following Jesus as He runs into the darkness to rescue the poor, the weak, the outcast, the widow and the orphan. May we discover, more and more, the joy of following You, Jesus.

DAY SEVEN JOURNAL ENTRY

On Sunday, the team preached and taught the healing model in five different churches. Following that, we went to what the locals call 'London'—the Nakuru city dump. This was my third time to 'London' and I was immediately struck by the absence of children. We found out that, since I had last been here a year earlier, Mike and his team have been able to get all but one of the children into boarding schools, where they can receive the education needed to break the generational cycle of poverty—good food, clean clothes and the empowerment of real hope. There was only one child left in the dump; one of the team sponsored this little boy and now he, too, is going to school. We had a chance to share Christ and pray for a sizable group of young men in their late teens and early 20's. All of them gave their hearts to Jesus. After that, we led an outdoor meeting in the community next to the dump; once again, many people were healed and saved. The team drove back to the hotel full of joy and amazed at all that the Lord had done on this very full day.

I know of nothing more rewarding, more exciting, more fulfilling than simply following Jesus as He runs into the darkness to rescue the poor, the weak, the outcast, the widow and the orphan.

5

INSIDE A JOURNEY OF COMPASSION: PART THREE

KENYA 2013: WHAT IS GOOD AND ETERNAL

This story is not a journal entry from the Kenya Journey; it was written at a later day, but it describes a key event that happened during that trip.

I was an hour outside of Nairobi, attending an African conference on disciple-making movements when we were informed that Somali terrorists had just attacked the Westgate Shopping Mall in Nairobi. Over the next forty-eight hours, over 225 innocent people would be killed or wounded. (That morning my wife, who was waiting for me in Nairobi decided to go shopping. Thankfully, she chose the other major shopping mall.) For the next couple of weeks, this story completely dominated the airwaves in Kenya. The outpouring of grief, shock, pain and anger was reminiscent of twelve years earlier in North America when the World Trade Center was attacked by terrorists. Indeed, the Westgate attack was Kenya's 9/11. This was the atmosphere into which our team arrived just 24 hours later.

Many months earlier we had planned a Journey of Compassion to Nakuru, a city of half a million about two hours west of Nairobi. Immediately upon our arrival, government leaders began to contact me, thanking us for deciding to go ahead with our mission trip, in spite of what had happened. To be honest, there was nothing I could have done to stop the trip at that point; twenty-five people were already on their way. On the first day of the Journey we were invited to plant ceremonial trees in the memorial park at the center of the city. This was a high honor, one not given to any other outside groups, conveying the government's thanks for us coming in the midst of their national tragedy. On several occasions, I found myself standing in front of television cameras and radio microphones, expressing our commitment to the Kenyan people, and assuring those from other nations that it was safe to come to Kenya.

The Westgate attack was Kenya's 9/11. This was the atmosphere into which our team arrived just 24 hours later.

The Westgate attack greatly heightened the ongoing mistrust and hatred between Somalia and Kenya. There is a long history of violence, but this attack was shocking in its ferocity. The emotions of the nation were exposed and volatile; yet in the midst of this, God surprised us mightily.

One morning during the second week of the Journey, while the team was gathered at the hotel for a time of worship and prayer, our partner Mike brought in a woman and asked us to pray for her. Two years earlier, she had been in a serious accident and had required surgery to insert a metal plate and pins. Since then, she had been constantly in great pain. As we gathered around and prayed for her, she started moving her limbs, then jumping up and down, shouting over and over, "It's gone! It's gone!"

When she left, we were rejoicing. Later, Mike told us that, in fact, that woman was the wife of the UN ambassador from Somalia. The next day, the ambassador telephoned Mike to say thanks and to

As we gathered around and prayed for her, she started moving her limbs, then jumping up and down, shouting over and over, "It's gone! It's gone!"

report that his wife was, indeed, completely healed. Knowing that the ambassador was one of the top leaders in a strictly Muslim nation, Mike asked whether or not it would be alright to let anyone know about his wife's healing. The ambassador replied, "Mike, Jesus Christ has healed my wife and you can tell the world."

This encounter was very significant prophetically. The enemy used terrorists from a cell in Somalia to inflict great pain, fear and anger in Kenya (the enemy always seeks to divide through conflict and mistrust), God responded by bringing healing to the wife of the ambassador, and doing it in Kenya. The enemy may rage, but the righteousness and mercy of God will prevail. Again—how was it that this small group of Impact Nations people could have been in the right place at the right time?

The movement of God is always toward restoration and reconciliation; that movement is relentless, inviting us to choose light in the midst of darkness, love where there seems to be only hatred, and hope instead of despair. Through the healing of the ambassador's wife, God brought a taste of His Kingdom to a nation greatly in need of something truly good and eternal.

6

INSIDE A JOURNEY OF COMPASSION: PART FOUR

KENYA 2013: FINAL JOURNAL ENTRY

I am sitting at Heathrow airport, waiting for a coach to take me to some leaders in Wales. So now there is time to contemplate all that we saw the Lord do in Kenya over the past two weeks.

If you have been following my reports, you know that the days were filled with healings, salvations and a series of divine encounters. I am deeply impressed by the timing of this Journey. As we were arriving, the worst terrorist attack in Kenya in 15 years was taking place. Suddenly, Kenya was at the center of the world's attention. In the midst of the deep anguish felt in this country, we found ourselves somehow speaking, not only to the nation, but to all of east Africa and indeed the world. For days afterwards, we heard from national leaders expressing their deep appreciation for what we shared on various television networks—that the world was praying for Kenya; that Kenya is a safe nation to visit;

that the people are warm and friendly, and that God's hand is on the nation. How does a small group of ordinary people from Canada, the UK and Australia have such a timely opportunity? Only the Lord could have made that happen.

Just before I got into the car to drive to the airport last night, Mike shared a wonderful report with us. Christina and the ladies led a women's conference last Saturday. For a week or two, her picture was on posters around Nakuru. There was a woman who, when she saw Christina's picture, told the Lord, "If that woman (Christina) will pray for me at the women's conference, I know that I will be healed of my HIV/AIDS." Last Saturday, Christina prayed for the woman. Yesterday, Mike received a call from her. She had undergone *seventeen* tests in hospitals in both Nakuru, then Nairobi. There is no trace of HIV/AIDS in her body!!

There was a woman who, when she saw Christina's picture, told the Lord, "If that woman (Christina) will pray for me at the women's conference, I know that I will be healed of my HIV/AIDS."

Yesterday, the team conducted a medical clinic at the city dump. Many were treated; many received healing prayer. In the midst of this, a local health care worker questioned our medical team leader about why we were there and what we were doing. This led to Mike calling her boss to make it clear that we had authority to do this. Then, something surprising happened. Near the end of the clinic, Mike received a call from the governor. He was calling all the way from China. He told Mike that he had been getting great reports about what Mike and the Impact Nations team had been doing in Nakuru. He expressed great appreciation for all that Mike does for the poor in the community. He then told Mike that he was *giving him a clinic!* As our medical leader said, this was like a gift dropping from heaven. This is a large, well equipped clinic where Mike can provide ongoing medical care for a community in desperate need. Once again, God did something amazing through our small act of care. If there was no Impact clinic in the dump yesterday, then no questions from the local worker, then no call to her boss, then no call to the governor's office, then no call to the governor in China, then no gift of a clinic. Once again, because of the Journey of Compassion, we had the privilege of being in the middle of something wonderful that God was doing. Who could have ever anticipated that?

I sometimes teach about the feeding of the 5,000. The disciples were faced with the seemingly impossible challenge of trying to feed this great throng with only a bit of fish and bread. It was as they gave away the bit that they had (no matter how inadequate it seemed) that God multiplied the food. This is a lesson that I keep learning at a deeper level—God will take whatever I have and multiply as I give it away. When we walk in the rhythm of the Kingdom, the Lord always seems to move with a mysterious, awesome acceleration and multiplication.

God will take whatever I have and multiply as I give it away.

So, why do we keep taking teams around the developing world? Because when we do, God always surprises us with His powerful love. Something is released that goes on and on long after we have returned home.

> *"You did not choose Me; I chose you and appointed you so that you might go and bear fruit—fruit that will last." (John 15:16)*

7

FINDING JESUS

It was 1989 and this was our first church plant. We were just a few weeks away from beginning to meet publicly on Sunday mornings, and I was determined that this new church would have care for the poor, the widow and the orphan as a core value; I was convinced that if we were truly going to follow Jesus, active and tangible expressions of His mercy must be in our foundation (Matthew 23:23). And so I went to the store to buy groceries, enough for about fifteen families. The next morning, our core group gathered at our house to distribute the hampers. We were all nervous; none of us had ever done this before and we were feeling very uncertain about what was waiting for us.

We went out in pairs, heading to what we assumed were poor neighborhoods. I think my knees were shaking as Joyce and I walked up to the first door. In hindsight, I'm sure our nervousness was obvious; it certainly did not help the recipients to feel more comfortable. We went to about four different homes, giving the food away and asking if we could pray for them. I don't really remember much of it. And then (finally and thankfully!) we were down to our last food hamper. At this house we encountered an elderly man named Frank. He kept insisting that he didn't want to buy our food. After several tries, he finally understood that we wanted to give the food to him. This crusty old man seemed very unimpressed by what was happening, but he did allow us to bring the food into his small home. When we asked if we could pray for him, Frank said, "I suppose so. If you like." As we started to pray the presence of the Lord filled the room. Suddenly, Frank embraced Joyce and began to weep. And weep. And weep.

I didn't know it at the time, but that day Jesus put a hook in my heart that has never come out. Without trying, without any sense of doing something magnanimous or spiritual, He had connected my heart with the poor. A year later, as the church was rapidly growing with people who were very excited to be engaged in Kingdom activity, we bought a bus and converted it to carry groceries and clothing. Twice a month, we took the "mercy bus" to various subsidized housing projects around our city. Over the years, we saw real and lasting change in a number of these neighborhoods. We went on to start "Saturday school" for the children; helped single mothers with household repairs; provided beds and other furniture for families in need; enjoyed many picnics and parties together; helped families through various crises; and saw families come to Jesus.

Six years later, the Lord clearly called us to Vancouver, Canada to plant another church. Again, we began to reach out to the poor as we were about to launch our Sunday morning service. Within a year or so, the church was connected to several housing projects in the city. It was exciting for me to see so many church members developing a lifestyle of helping and encouraging poor families, typically headed by a single mother. Besides our corporate outings to bring food, fun and prayer to these families, many individuals opened their hearts and lives in creative ways—free haircuts, a weekly children's activity time that gave the mothers a break and introduced the children to Jesus, and Christmas parties where each child in the complex received a personal gift that was purchased especially for them, along with a Christmas meal.

In the midst of this, I felt the Lord calling me to a deeper personal journey of following Him in serving the "least of these brethren." I began to set apart a block of time each week when I would leave the church office and go downtown, to the poorest areas of our city. Over the years I took lunches to men and women living alone in filthy flophouses, food to street people, and hot drinks to prostitutes working the streets at night. My journey sometimes took me under a number of the city's bridges, where some of the most desperate people huddled out of the rain. I got to know people by name, and was able to spend time with them week by week. I met people whose bodies were being attacked by AIDS. I got to know good people who were trapped by their addiction to drugs and alcohol. I met runaways, men and women suffering with mental illness, and some who it seemed had simply suffered a series of hard breaks.

I hesitated to write the previous paragraph because I realize that it could draw attention to me doing "good works". But that is not the point. The point is Matthew 25: 31-40. I wasn't taking Jesus to these broken people; Jesus was already there. I think He was waiting for me. There was

I wasn't taking Jesus to these broken people; Jesus was already there.

nothing noble in anything I did; I was simply responding to Jesus calling me, wooing me out of my false sense of security and comfort. Through these men, women and teenagers, Jesus was ministering to me, healing my heart, changing the boundaries of the Gospel, and opening my eyes to how each of these people, in various ways, were a mirror to remind me of my own great need and of His great grace.

Like so many people, my life's direction has come as a great surprise. (I suppose John Lennon was right when he wrote that life is what happens to you while you are busy making other plans.) Amazingly, doors have opened for me in some of the poorest countries and communities in the world. Somehow, I get to participate in bringing clean water, food, medicine and employment opportunities to those in desperate situations. I am allowed to see families and even whole communities being transformed by practical demonstrations of the love of Christ. Many times I find myself asking Him, *Why do I get to do these things?* I know it is all His grace and mercy to me, but I think I hear Him telling me that, at least in part, it is because of the years when I let Him stretch me, break my heart, and discover Him among the poor.

If I could, I would tell everyone that to spend our lives on the poor is no burden. Neither is it noble. Rather, it is a great privilege, and sometimes a great joy. After all, that is where Jesus is.

> *"He gave justice and help to the poor and needy, and everything went well for him. Isn't that what it means to know me?" says the LORD. (Jeremiah 22:16)*

8

WHEN GOD BROKE IN

When I'm on my own I like the unexpected; I am made for spontaneity. But I readily confess that when responsible for a group of people, I prefer to have a well-defined plan and to know what is happening. So as we headed two hours north from Manila, I was aware of a growing discomfort. We were headed to Pampanga, an area in the Philippines totally new to us, working with people whom we had not previously met. As our bus drove the last mile toward where we were about to set up our mobile medical clinic, the signs of serious poverty were obvious. This community was known for prostitution, drugs and gambling—the kind of place that found its energy at night and, except for the children who seemed to be everywhere, slept during the day.

With this in mind, I expected a slow start to the clinic. I was wrong. As we approached the site, we couldn't even get near the courtyard because of the press of people waiting impatiently. There was a problem: contrary to our arrangements, nothing had been set up. After much shouting, jostling and more than a little frustration, we finally cleared out the courtyard and were able to organize tables, chairs, assessment areas and a pharmacy. An hour later, an already tired and rather jangled team was ready to see the first patient. While our medical and prayer teams began to care for the people, I walked among the crowds to offer reassurance and to lower the level of anxiety that could so easily be felt. So often—and for good reason—the poor live with a deep fear of missing out.

In the early afternoon a seven-year-old boy named Dennis came to me with his cousin tagging behind. He proclaimed: "Hey mister, this is my cousin Angelica. She's nine. She can't hear anything. She's never heard anything. You need to pray for her." This was no shy request; this was a command born of total confidence. So I prayed for Angelica's ears to open. Who would say no to *this* boy? Nothing happened. I prayed again. Still nothing. After a third time, I sent Dennis away but encouraged him to come back later. I felt confused, frustrated and deeply sad for Angelica. After all, I know that Jesus loves to heal. This boy had come with obvious faith, and I had prayed, fully expecting her ears to open, as I had seen the Lord do so many times before.

This was no shy request; this was a command born of total confidence.

Later in the afternoon, I took a few team members and some local pastors out on the streets. Everyone we prayed for received healing. Some of the team prayed for an older man who had not been able to stand for over four years. First the pain in his legs, hips and back left completely, then he stood and, after a moment, he took his first steps. A crowd immediately gathered, eager for prayer. A mother's two children were instantly healed and as she excitedly told everyone her story, another woman's chest pain left. A woman who had experienced pain in her shoulder for four months left with no pain—but not before opening her heart to Jesus. As team members prayed on the streets, numerous people came to Christ. At one point two women worked their way to the front of the small crowd that had gathered in an alleyway, to ask us if they too could invite Jesus into their lives; it was a joy to lead them in a salvation prayer.

Like everyone, I rejoiced to see so many healed and saved. But even in the midst of this heavenly breakthrough, one question remained: What about Angelica?

Our team came back excited that evening, prepared to conduct an outdoor celebration on the street, with music, preaching and praying for the sick. As we approached the site, it was clear that something was wrong. Where were the people? Where was the local worship band? Where was the sound system? As we stood waiting on the side of the road, children began to gather around us. Within a couple of minutes there was a crowd of them, excitedly anticipating that something special was about to happen on their poor street. I confess that instead of feeling excitement, once again I was fighting frustration as I saw my plans to preach the Gospel to the people of this community dissolve away.

Some of our team, better able to appreciate the moment than I, began to dance and sing with the children. In the meantime someone showed up with a microphone and speaker. By now there were about one hundred very enthusiastic, happy children. Finally it dawned on me: God was wonderfully at work on this street; it just looked different than what I had envisioned. I asked two of our team, ChaCha and Rebekah (who is a gifted puppeteer), to talk to the kids using the microphone. Before long AJ, Rebekah's puppet friend—who seemed more human by the moment— and ChaCha were telling the children about Jesus. Nearly all of the children raised their hands to receive Him, with AJ leading the prayer.

But the Lord had saved the best until last. As we began to pray for the children, Angelica's little cousin Dennis once again pulled her by the hand toward me. "Hey Mister, you pray for my cousin now?" Just as I was about to pray, I sensed the Lord directing me to ask Rebekah to come over, which she did—with AJ. As Rebekah prayed, suddenly Angelica's startled eyes opened wide. Something was happening. Angelica's head began to turn this way and that as she heard the sound of people speaking all around her. When Rebekah and I repeatedly spoke and snapped our fingers behind her head, Angelica heard every sound. A minute later, she spoke her first words. Now Angelica and Dennis were calling back and forth to each other, stepping further apart each time, laughing with unbridled joy. I will never forget that sight. If there were any dry eyes, I certainly didn't see them. Later, a very excited team drove home, thanking God for what He had done. More than just a miracle of healing, a little girl's entire life had just been transformed in a moment.

Among my experiences of miraculous healing all over the world, perhaps none has stayed with me more than what the

More than just a miracle of healing, a little girl's entire life had just been transformed in a moment.

Lord did that night. The love and devotion of that little boy for his cousin and his unrelenting quest for her to receive healing continues to teach me to not quit and to choose to live with the expectation that God is about to break in at any moment.

9

YOUR ARM IS NOT TOO SHORT

I have been home from Haiti for only a few days. Once again the sights, sounds and memories seem to swirl in my head like a recently shaken snow globe. Even more than most trips, this one was marked by a remarkable number of healings and miracles—in fact, too many to keep track of. Blind eyes opened, those born deaf heard, chronic pain—some of it lasting for years and years—suddenly and completely vanished.

How can anyone describe the emotional impact of a blind grandmother receiving her sight and then, for the first time, seeing the face of her grandson? I look at a photo of this elderly woman laughing as she gazes at the boy, while her daughter weeps tears of joy. This is real. It is as though the stories that I have read in the pages of the Bible for years have come to life and invited me to join in.

Another image comes to mind. We are in one of the mobile medical clinics. A young man in his early twenties who has been deaf and mute since birth receives prayer from two women on our team. Suddenly, he begins to look around wide-eyed, responding to the first sounds he has ever heard. I am happy, but quickly I turn back to what I was doing in the clinic. Then a shout goes up as this young man begins to speak his first words. I can hear his loud voice clearly over what is now a small crowd as he shouts, "Hallelujah!" The ladies continue to speak words to him and each time, he repeats them, clearly and confidently. Jesus, how do You do this? The next day, this young man comes to the church where some of our team were ministering. He is overheard telling a person who is making hand signs to him that there is no need to gesture; "I'm not deaf anymore," he says.

Now I am remembering Thursday morning and we are in a crowded marketplace. While we spread out to offer to pray for people, one of our team stands up on a small mound and begins to preach. He has never preached outside before, but he has been emboldened by all that he has seen Jesus do around and through him these past few days. And so he preaches. And the people stop what they are doing and listen. Some immediately give their lives to Christ. All at once, he is aware that the Lord's presence and power are there in a mighty way to heal. Almost as fast as he and others from the team touch those in pain, they are healed. A great cheer rises that I can hear from the other end of the market. I immediately think of Mark's Gospel where he writes that the people brought the sick and the lame to Jesus in the marketplace and He healed them all (Mark 6:56). He is still working in the marketplace.

There are so many images: time and again we watch as eyes blurred by cataracts are instantly healed; a damaged eye, milky white, begins to change before us as a dark pupil and iris are formed by the hand of the Lord; a small boy, his leg in a metal brace, is carried to us and then after prayer he walks away while his mother holds the leg brace in her hands. Over the twelve days of the Journey, how many were healed of pain, sickness and fever? How many lumps disappeared? How many heard and saw clearly for the first time? Only You know, Jesus. What You did was beyond our capacity to comprehend or even keep up with.

A damaged eye, milky white, begins to change before us as a dark pupil and iris are formed by the hand of the Lord.

Once again, while I am thousands of miles from the familiar, You teach me.

It is hot as we walk along the dirt path that runs beside a canal where boys are swimming. As the only white people in this remote community, we are somewhat of a curiosity; soon, we are being followed by a crowd. As is our custom everywhere we go, we ask if anyone needs to be healed. Immediately we are surrounded by both the curious and the desperate. One after another is healed. A small, naked boy climbs out of the canal and pushes his way through the crowd. His mother steps up and explains that he has been deaf and mute since birth. One of the team begins to pray for the boy, when suddenly he looks down, realizes that he is naked, and runs off down the path as fast as he can go. To our surprise, two minutes later he comes running back, this time with shorts on. We pray for his ears to be opened. Nothing happens. We pray again. Nothing. The boy smiles at us and then, once again, runs away.

A few minutes later, as we walk back to our bus, I share with a team member that, no matter how often I see the Lord heal people, I always feel pain when a person is not healed. For a long time now, I have been convinced that this pain is the number one reason why the Western church does not pray for the sick. I was delighted with all the healing that He did do, but still the mystery of why the deaf boy was not healed lingers. As I sit on the bus thinking about all that has transpired, our scattered team comes back from all directions, followed by lots of children. A couple of minutes later I hear a commotion outside the bus and go to investigate. Two of our ladies had seen this same little deaf boy and decided to pray for him. After only a moment of prayer, his eyes had begun to look all around. One of the ladies had stood behind him and whispered, "Jesus". This child who had never in his life heard a sound, called back, "Jesus". Although, as the first word he had ever said, it was somewhat slurred, with each new word, his speech became clearer. Now, for the first time, the boy notices the music coming from the bus we are on and he begins to move and dance to its rhythm. A very happy, thankful and deeply contented team heads back our home base!

How often do I miss what the Lord is doing and therefore quit too soon? I have spent years teaching people about recognizing God's activity amongst and around us. I have explained that His angels are constantly on assignment (just as Jacob saw for himself near Bethel). I have declared that all prayer must ultimately effect change (Luke 18:7). Yet,

I had looked at a little boy, seemingly still deaf after we prayed for him, and determined that God had not healed him. Thankfully, others persevered.

I have heard it said that prayer is like the law of gravity: "What goes up, must come down." While I was walking along, embracing my disappointment, God's Spirit was at work in that little boy's body.

Prayer is like the law of gravity: "What goes up, must come down."

Hundreds of years before Jesus' birth, the prophet Isaiah looked across the centuries and declared of Him:

He will not judge by what he sees with his eyes,
or decide by what he hears with his ears;
but with righteousness he will judge the needy,
with justice he will give decisions for the poor of the
    earth. (Isaiah 11:3-5 NIV)

Satan has tried many times to stop me from praying for the sick and needy by telling me that my prayers accomplish nothing. How often have I agreed with him: "That's right. Nothing happened."? But the One who continually invites me to follow Him never agreed with Satan. This is why Jesus did not judge the activity of heaven by what He saw or heard in the natural, but rather by embracing what He saw His Father doing.

Jesus, keep teaching me to do what You do, to see what You see, and to hear what You hear. And while I am in the midst of the battle, keep me trusting You.

10

MY LOVE AFFAIR WITH INDIA

There is no other nation on earth like India—its cities offer a sensory overload of sounds, sights and smells. To walk down any street is to experience hundreds of horns honking at once, the shouts of shopkeepers trying to attract passersby, the pervasive aromas of exotic mixtures of spices, and *everywhere* the press of people. Often the first day, Westerners discover they either love India or they hate it. I am definitely in the first category.

And then there are the villages. Gandhi called them the real India. One eighth of the world's population lives in a village in India. Going there is like stepping back in time, where life has gone on essentially without change for hundreds of years (except for the ubiquitous cell phones). The women head out to the fields to work without machinery, in the same way their ancestors did centuries ago. It is a hard life, making women look twenty or thirty years older than they really are. Often I have been the first white person that any of the villagers have seen. Once, I took two friends from California into a village. A woman asked my friend where he was from.

When he replied, the United States, she asked—"Is that past Hubli?" (a town about an hour away). To walk through a remote village in India is to seemingly enter another world.

Beginning with my first trip to India in 1997, my heart was captured. Here's how it happened: I had been in Delhi for several days when I was asked to go to a seminary two hours away to teach the students. As my new friend Leslie and I drove along, he asked if we could make a detour into a village for a few minutes so he could do some business there. This was fine with me, as I had been looking forward to seeing an Indian village. I got out of the car and waited for him in the dirt lane. In just a couple of minutes, about 40 villagers silently gathered in front of me. As the minutes went by, I felt whiter and whiter. While I was standing there in an increasing state of discomfort, I sensed the Lord point out to me a boy with a bandage on his head, and then He told me to pray for him. Now this was really getting awkward. Without a common language, what would he think if I just walked over and started to pray? So I asked the Lord, "Pray for him for what?" He answered with silence. Now I was really squirming. So, taking a deep breath, I walked over to the boy and prayed. Nothing happened.

While I was pondering what had just taken place, Leslie came around the corner. As he walked up to me, I suddenly found myself calling out to the small crowd, "If anyone here needs healing today, Jesus Christ the Son of God will heal you." Never before had I done anything like that, and truthfully I was somewhat horrified at what I had just said. Immediately, however, a middle-aged man came forward. He told me (Leslie now provided me with ears and a voice), that he couldn't lift his arms because of the pain. In response, I told him, "It is Jesus Christ who heals you," and then prayed. He began to shout and raise his arms high over his head. A woman now stood in front of me and said she too needed healing. Instantly she was healed. Then the next person. And the next. As each person was healed, I told them that it was Jesus who was healing them. Soon there were at least 100 people there. For about 90 minutes Jesus healed person after person. The crowd got more and more excited.

Finally, Leslie insisted that we had to go, because we were now very late for the seminary appointment. I remember as I was getting into the car, another woman ran to me and grabbed my coat, refusing to let go until I prayed for her. She too was healed instantly. As we drove away, Leslie asked me, "Did you hear what there were all saying?" Of course not; I couldn't understand Hindi. He then told me, "They were saying over and over to each other, 'It is Jesus Christ, the Son of God who is healing!'"

This was my very first experience in a Hindu village. It was also the first time I had seen so much healing break out, and for such a long time. Obviously, Leslie and I were rejoicing all the way to the seminary. (Over the years, the irony of leaving what the Lord was doing in that village to go to talk to seminary students about what He does, has never left me.)

What happened in that village seemed to open the door for the next three weeks to a series of miracles all over northern India. I traveled with believers for a week, then with three

Hindu men for two more weeks. Wherever we went, we saw
Jesus heal—in shops, factories, restaurants, even in a Hindu
ashram. And it all started when
I stepped out in spite of my
great discomfort and prayed
for the boy with a bandage.
God released something
through that simple act.

*It all started when I
stepped out in spite of
my great discomfort and
prayed for the boy…*

• • •

There is a coda to this story. Seven weeks after I returned
home to Canada, I received a phone call from a pastor in
India. He had visited that same village two nights earlier. He
called to tell me that even more people had been healed that
day, nearly two months ago, than I could ever have known.
He told me of children who had been dying of dysentery who
were instantly healed, of the deaf who could now hear, and of
many more healings. But the real reason he called was to tell
me what he had discovered happening in that Hindu village.
The people now gathered regularly to pray for the sick and
for one another in the name of Jesus, the Son of God.

Remember how, in the midst of praying for the sick, I was
suddenly pulled away into the car *without the opportunity
to preach the Gospel*. But that did not limit the Lord. In
the midst of the miracles, He revealed Himself. There are
so many lessons to be learned by what happened in that
village. Twice Jesus said in John's Gospel, that if we have
trouble believing who He is, believe in the miracles because
they point to Him (John 10:38; 14:11). Clearly, this is what

happened. He also said in Mark 1:15, "The Kingdom of God is here. Repent and believe." I think Jesus was saying that if people experience the Kingdom, their hearts will be turned to Him. This Gospel that we carry so powerfully heals and transforms, that it will do its work even without us.

The Gospel itself is the power of God unto salvation (Romans 1:16).

Amen and amen.

11

SURPRISED AGAIN

I remember it like it happened yesterday. It was early evening in a poor neighborhood, a slum really, in Nakuru, Kenya, during the second week of our Journey of Compassion. People, curious about the music and preaching, had gathered in a dusty and dirty field surrounded by dilapidated shacks. Considering how the Lord had been moving so powerfully during this entire Journey, I shouldn't have been surprised with what He was about to do.

Beginning the first day, when 460 people gave their lives to Christ in a downtown park, this had been a remarkable Journey where God kept showing up in ways that surprised us.

Sometimes the Lord moves faster than what we are ready for. At the beginning of this Journey, just as we were settling into a day of teaching and training at the hotel, we were told to get ready to go downtown. Nakuru is a city of about a half million and the city officials had decided to throw Impact Nations a parade. "A *what?*" I asked. "A parade. Quick, get ready. It will be fun!" In thirty minutes we were being led by a marching band right through the middle of downtown to the central park, where each team member was going to plant a ceremonial tree. Maybe it was a slow day, because with every block we walked, more and more people followed. At this point perhaps I should talk about how excited I was to see this great opportunity for the Gospel forming, but that's not true. I was just feeling a bit embarrassed at all the attention. (I am a Canadian, after all.)

As we reached the park, my Kenyan friend said, "Steve, look at all these people. Get up on the truck and start preaching. Keep it short; you've got their attention right now." Magically, a microphone appeared and I started preaching—three minutes, tops. Then I invited people to come forward to the truck if they needed to

"Steve, look at all these people. Get up on the truck and start preaching. Keep it short; you've got their attention right now."

give their lives to Jesus. Not only did the crowd in front of me respond, they came from all around, wherever my words had been heard. I was told of one man later who was in a store buying a pair of pants when he heard me. He felt like something was pulling him to the park. Mike, who the reader might remember from "Inside a Journey" previously, invited the people who came forward to leave their names and contact information. Amazingly, 460 people did just that, and Mike's team later followed up with all of them. What a start to the Journey!

Over the following days we saw many Muslims joyfully turn to Jesus as we brought clean water to a Masai village for the first time; as we treated hundreds in the mobile medical clinics; and as we watched the Lord graciously heal hundreds of people.

•   •   •

It was now a week later. The day was quickly giving way to night as we found ourselves standing in a large empty lot in one of the poorest neighborhoods in Nakuru. Men and women, returning from the market or a long day of work, were crisscrossing the field, paying very little attention to us. Once the music began to blare across the area, people began to gather. I thought I was preaching that night, but to my surprise while I was speaking with people out on the field, I heard one of the team members begin to preach to the steadily growing crowd. As she spoke, the Holy Spirit began to move powerfully. At the back of the crowd, some of the team began to lay hands on those who couldn't see because of severe cataracts. Suddenly, everyone they touched was being healed. There was a growing excitement as person after person exclaimed that they could see. The Lord's presence continued to increase. The deaf heard; pain left; fevers vanished. But even more, there was an awareness among those gathered that God was in our midst, that this was a holy time and a holy place. Many came forward to ask Jesus into their lives, to receive the gift of a new beginning. And still they came, first the old, then

There was an awareness among those gathered that God was in our midst, that this was a holy time and a holy place.

the young men and women. When our Impact Nations team finally left, it was with a sense of awe because of what we had seen and experienced of the Lord's goodness.

Now, more than a year later, a church has been established amongst these people. Almost all who attend are new believers. More than 2,000 people gather there every week. What the Lord began that night has continued to flourish and grow. Through the vision and hard work of my Kenyan friend and his team, men and women are leaving abject poverty behind as they learn new job skills and are helped to start small businesses. The community is changing.

Surprised again. As the years go by, I am slowly learning that God's surprises always lead to something that lasts, that transforms a seemingly hopeless situation. I suppose that's why Jesus went out of His way to tell us to learn to hear what the Father is saying, to see what He is doing and then get on board. Because more than anyone I know, God seems to love surprises.

12

HAITI 2010: A DEVASTATING EARTHQUAKE

They were two days that I will never forget. Never.

I was in the midst of a five-nation scouting tour in Africa, checking out potential Journeys of Compassion and various projects. While I was in Africa, my wife Christina and one of our spiritual sons, Adam LiVecchi, were in Carrefour, Haiti, on their own scouting trip for Impact Nations. Several days into the trip, I was awakened by my cell phone in the very early hours of the morning. When I opened the text message, I was confronted with this from my wife:

Earthquake. Adam and I okay. Don't know what to do.

As I woke up, I remember thinking that Christina was talking about some kind of major spiritual shakeup, like a revival breaking out. But as I re-read her text, the truth sunk in. I responded:

Get to the embassy as quickly as you can.

A few moments later, she replied,

Can't move. Don't know what to…

At that moment, all communication between Haiti and the outside world was cut off.

At 4:55 pm on Tuesday, January 12, 2010, Haiti had just suffered one of the most catastrophic earthquakes of the last hundred years world-wide. In thirty-eight seconds, nearly 300,000 people were killed, as buildings collapsed in cities all over the western and southern part of the country. But for the next two days, I confess I was mainly thinking about two people—Christina and Adam. I kept trying to push down the panic I felt at her final message. *Can't move. Don't know what to...* I knew that Haiti had the potential to be dangerous in normal times (that is why I asked Adam to travel with Christina); what must it be like in the midst of all the chaos? Then, on the morning of the second day, I was contacted and told that Christina had officially been registered as a missing person by the Canadian embassy.

For two days, in order to emotionally cope, all I could do was pray and keep busy. I continued to travel to various communities and preach as scheduled. While I preached, the fear seemed to lift; as soon as I stopped, it came back with a vengeance. Later on the second day (was it really only two days? It honestly seemed like at least five!), while we were driving to another city, my phone beeped and this is what I read:

On way to airport. All safe. Miracles continue...big crowds...We both could have been killed. The house is destroyed. All 25 safe. Many angels.

I seem to recall being aware that I was laughing and crying all at once. Never before had I felt such relief. It took another day to find out what had happened. I will let Christina tell it in her own words:

4:53 p.m. I was sitting on my bed in a second floor bedroom of the pastor's house, working on my computer. Suddenly I was bombarded by a sound unlike anything I had ever heard—like a thousand jet planes taking off all around me. Immediately the room began to shake violently. What was happening was unmistakable. The walls began to rip apart like paper, then the entire house collapsed under me. Miraculously, the roof over my head did not come down. Less than a minute later I heard Adam calling my name as he ran to my room. (Later I learned that when the earthquake began, Adam instinctively jumped out of his bed just before a concrete wall collapsed onto it.) With our eyes and throats choked with dust, we made our way to the next room where the outside walls were blown out. We climbed through the opening and onto a tree; helped by two young men, we made our way down to the ground. Immediately, I texted Steve in Kenya. My first text went through, but the second was cut off in the middle. From then on my cell phone didn't work.

Within an hour, the entire lot around what was left of the house was filled with the crush of thousands of people—all of them in shock. I will always remember the image of a man holding his baby up in the air and repeatedly saying, "Merci, Jesu". We were thankful to be alive. Soon it was pitch black. The lot was so packed with people, in this, the only open space available, that we could not move or even sit down. All night there were aftershocks; with each one, the crowd screamed in terror and more buildings collapsed.

Just before 3 a.m., a flood of people ran by on the road shouting, "La mer! La mer!" A rumor had started that a tsunami was coming. Suddenly the crowd all around me was in a panic, and a stampede to higher ground began. I had no choice but to run too, with Adam and Jordan, a young Haitian man who never left my side throughout the ordeal. As we ran in pitch darkness along rubble-strewn streets, this was my first glimpse of the neighborhood. Almost nothing was left standing. The sight of such universal devastation was shocking; it was hard to take in what I was seeing. After about ten or fifteen minutes, the stampede stopped; everyone realized that, in fact, there was no wave coming.

All night there were aftershocks; with each one, the crowd screamed in terror and more buildings collapsed.

For the next two days, we stayed on the lot, with no water, food or toilets. On the morning after the second night, Pastor Eddy put us in his SUV and we headed toward the airport. Death and destruction were everywhere. We finally arrived at the airport only to discover that it, too, was unsafe. While I waited with the crowd, wondering what to do, a Haitian-Canadian with a car invited me to drive with her to the Canadian embassy. After a few hours there, I was taken to the airport. That night, I was flown out on the first Hercules airplane that the Canadian air force had sent to Haiti.

As the ground heaved, structures everywhere gave way. In a moment, 1.3 million people were made homeless. Power was cut off; pipes were broken, contaminating the water. As so often happens following natural disasters, a week or two later, cholera and typhoid broke out around the country. And of course, hunger was rampant.

Only three weeks later, Adam went to the Dominican Republic, the country on the eastern side of the island shared with Haiti. Relief funds had been coming into Impact Nations every day, and so Adam was able to drive across the country for 18 hours with a truck filled with food, supplies and medicine. Returning to Carrefour, Adam told me that it was like driving in a war zone. Everywhere, there were collapsed buildings; many others were teetering at weird angles, on the verge of falling down. Most streets were impassible, with huge mounds of rubble blocking the way. As they drove through Carrefour, crowds of people called out to them for help. Even as they distributed over two thousand pounds of food, the fear and agitation among the people were unmistakable. Adam was very thankful for the presence of the US Marines who were in Carrefour to help distribute food and water, and to try to keep the peace.

Returning to Carrefour, Adam told me that it was like driving in a war zone.

Upon his return to the United States, Adam called me and spoke about the need for us to go back in with a large team. I agreed, and so we announced a Journey of Compassion; fifty people from nations all over the world came together to bring practical and supernatural help, healing and comfort to the most devastated place I ever hope to see.

What follows this chapter are three stories based upon

my journal entries and reports from that first Journey. You will note that there is a certain element of repetition to these. It is intentional. My aim was to reinforce to the reader the remarkable impact, in many ways, that post-earthquake Haiti assaulted the senses. It is my hope that somehow, some way, you, the reader, will get a sense of what it was like to be there.

Since that first unforgettable Journey to Haiti, I have been back many times, both on my own, and with Impact Nations teams. Each time, the mountains of rubble were smaller, until they were largely gone (something I had thought could never happen). There is still a problem with permanent housing for over 300,000 people. The "temporary" tent cities are places of frustration and growing hopelessness. Even five years later, articles are still being written about where all the relief money has gone. From what I have seen and experienced, it seems clear that it is the small, quickly mobile and adaptable organizations that have been able to respond to the crisis most effectively. I am pleased that Impact Nations has been one of many such groups. I am aware of so much great work continuing to be done in this, the poorest nation in the Western hemisphere.

We have gone back to Carrefour, where a church rose up out of the pain of those first months; it continues to grow, to train disciples and to plant other churches in far-off communities. We have been to cities in the north and south. We have traveled to remote villages, bringing the Good News of salvation, healing, and practical demonstrations of the love of Jesus. We have seen the impact of clean water on entire communities, of medical care, of tens of thousands of meals for children, of small businesses started, and of a school. It has been a joy to watch as Jesus has healed thousands and thousands of people.

In the midst of the confusion, false starts, miscommunication, and profoundly different ways of doing things, I love Haiti and I love the Haitian people—but not as much as Jesus does.

13

HAITI 2010: FROM MY JOURNAL: THE FIRST DAYS

Christina and I have been here about 10 hours now. We flew in today from New York. Immediately upon leaving the airport I was struck by the fact that around me are people who are missing arms and legs as a result of the earthquake. Very slowly, we worked our way through the labyrinth of blocked and broken streets. It is quite an experience seeing countless buildings lying as masses of rubble. We inched by the huge presidential palace, now cracked and broken, with the front half leaning crazily like some giant metaphor of what has happened to this nation. Everywhere are the signs of terrible suffering and deprivation. As we drive, we are told that there is no one who hasn't lost family in the earthquake.

As we drive, we are told that there is no one who hasn't lost family in the earthquake.

A few hours later, I went to an outdoor meeting with Pastor Eddy. I thought that I was going to observe, but instead, I found myself preaching. We were in a field by the sea, strewn with rubble left over from the quake. There were about 1,000 people there, even though a rather spectacular lightning show was taking place (with, of course, the threat of rain). After speaking, I named a few specific maladies that I sense the Lord was about to heal, then had those people stand and had the person beside them pray with me for them. God healed too many to count. Among the testimonies was a woman who had been born completely deaf in her right ear (she looked about 60). Jesus totally healed her. As Pastor Eddy tested her hearing by speaking softer and softer, she repeated everything perfectly (I couldn't hear what he was saying by the end!). The crowd cheered mightily. Another testimony: A man who, for four years, had been in so much pain that he had been unable to work, was now pain free.

•   •   •

The next day:

At 6:30 this morning, hundreds of people started to gather under the shade of large trees by the seaside. The church service began at seven. Church gatherings always happen early in the morning or in the evening—the heat makes anything else impossible. The natural setting was spectacular, with the Caribbean off to my right as I spoke from a high platform. But looking straight ahead, beyond the crowd, I was struck with the contrast: behind the crowd lay the collapsed ruins of what had been the city's major sports stadium.

The Haitians are a people that, naturally speaking, have been overtaken by destruction. Everywhere are destroyed buildings, hills of rubble, people now living shoulder to shoulder in tents and under tarps. However, what I heard today at this "outdoor cathedral" was the sound of joy and thankfulness. With the eyes of faith, they see a totally new kind of Haiti rising from the destruction of the old one. They are convinced that God will give them what they ask for: justice and healing for the land, righteousness, integrity and prosperity. I heard it in their songs, their testimonies and their prayers.

Near the end of the service, people began to come forward and give testimonies of the healing that the Lord did at last night's meeting. A line formed as one person after another clearly shared about being healed. A woman who had suffered constant head pain since she was a teenager was suddenly and completely pain free. A man who had an accident 6 years ago and had severe pain in his leg since then, danced before the church and shouted with joy that all pain was gone. These kinds of testimonies went on for a long time. Because of the size of the crowd last night, I had simply asked them to put their hand over wherever the pain was, and then I prayed for healing from the platform. Jesus did an amazing work at this first gathering. I wonder just how much healing we will see in the next 12 days? I can hardly wait to meet with the team and prepare them to move among the sick of Carrefour.

On Sunday night about 6,000 gathered! Once again healing broke out everywhere.

After all that had taken place during the first night, the word went out through Carrefour that healing was happening. I spoke on Saturday evening to a crowd of about 1,000-1,500. On Sunday night about 6,000 gathered! Once again healing broke out everywhere. The response was singing and dancing that went on and on.

> *"The entire crowd rejoiced at all the wonderful things Jesus was doing." (Luke 13:17)*

14

HAITI 2010: FROM MY JOURNAL: THREE DAYS IN CARREFOUR

As I write this, the skies have opened up again. The rain has a force, almost a violence to it. Nothing seems to happen in this country in moderation. Driving in Carrefour is a slow process, as the traffic has to weave its way between great mounds of rubble; some streets are still completely blocked. Countless numbers of buildings lie in ruins, simply great slabs of concrete, and cement dust. Others are still standing, but tilted at strange angles as if waiting to fall over at any moment. The city is filled with tent cities where families are packed into impossibly tight spaces—we have been told there are still 500,000 people without a place to live. Yesterday I saw a man curled up on a pile of rubble not 5 feet from the loud, busy traffic; he was sleeping with some rags wrapped around him. The main streets are filled with people on the move. Everyone is looking for a way to either make some money or find something they can purchase.

On Wednesday we began our first mobile medical clinics.

We have a large team of nurses, a dentist, paramedics and a doctor. The first day was very difficult. Some key pieces were accidentally left behind at the hotel. By the time we retrieved them, we had lost 90 minutes of clinic time. Yet when I addressed the crowd, to my great surprise (and relief), they were not frustrated, but thankful, shouting out 'Hallelujah' and 'Merci'. I joked with them, "Is this a medical clinic or a church meeting?" But as the hours go by, the heat began to take its toll on some of them. In their desperation, many of the people were afraid of missing out. (Again, this is so common among the really poor all over the world.) After a hard day, we have only seen about 100 people. The team went home tired but determined to see more the next day.

It is Thursday and everything has changed. We provided medicine and vitamins to more people than ever before–750 people! While the people waited under the tarps, different team members preached to them about the love of Jesus and how He loves to heal. Many came to faith in Him; many more are healed as they waited. At the end of a long day, we went back to the hotel happy and thankful to have seen so many people.

•   •   •

Now it is Friday. Earlier, some of the team went to a school and spent time with the children. Others went to two tent cities. I have been among the very poor in many developing countries, but I have never seen such despair and terrible living conditions as at the first tent city. The tents were so close together that in most cases it was impossible to pass between them. There is no pattern, simply a chaotic maze. They are simply hot vinyl covers with a few sticks as poles and dirt floors. Whenever it rains (like right now), rivers of mud and water flow through the tents. There was no sound of children laughing or people visiting—just hollow, vacant expressions. It is so easy to feel overwhelmed.

From there we went to a second tent city, this one set up by the French. Here, the tents were more spaced out (perhaps a foot or two between them) and they were set up in rows. But the camp has been situated near the sea, at the bottom of the hill on which Carrefour is built. As a result, whenever it rained, the garbage and sewage of the city flowed directly into this tent city. When we asked people how we could pray, besides various pains and sicknesses (which the Lord so often healed), we heard the cry of people who simply wanted their life back. We met with Greg, a young leader in this community. We asked how we could help in some way. Greg showed us an area where the children played and then asked if we could level it for soccer and volleyball. He also asked if we could dig some drainage ditches around the tents. Two hours later, team members were back with shovels, rakes, pick-axes and a couple of wheelbarrows. As we unloaded the tools, the people gathered to ask if they could help. In no time, men, women and children were working hard on the field in about 40 degree heat (that's 105 F). They worked hard and enthusiastically. Before long, we were helping them as they

We heard the cry of people who simply wanted their life back.

led the way. While we worked, they asked if we would stay and conduct a worship meeting. We hadn't even told them who we were, so we were surprised at the request.

After our work was done for the day, our team gathered beside the tents and began to worship. Immediately, people gathered. With our translators, we sang in both English and Creole. More and more people joined in with both singing and dancing. As we worshiped, something caught my eye: 400 yards away, standing on a roof, was a man swaying to the music with his arms raised in worship to the Lord. It was an image I won't easily forget. After a while, two of our young team members began to preach; immediately, there was a strong sense of God's presence. It was as though, right there in the midst of the despair and poverty of the tent city, we had stepped onto holy ground. A number of people gave their hearts to Jesus. We prayed for the sick until it was quite dark; once again, to the delight of everyone, Jesus healed many.

15

HAITI 2010: SOME FINAL THOUGHTS

We saw too many miracles to count during this Journey of Compassion. Jesus was healing everywhere we went— during the medical clinics, while helping with recovery projects, along the streets, in the tent cities. Because the rainy season had started, with some epic thunderstorms, we were only able to conduct four outdoor healing and evangelism meetings. However, each of these was exciting. The Lord healed many on the first night, and so the good news quickly spread. The meetings grew to over 5,000 people. One night, in about an hour, I conservatively estimated that a thousand people were healed. Just after we started to pray for the crowd, a huge rainstorm suddenly broke out. As some of the hardest rain I had ever seen pounded down, no one left. Instead they cheered, and waited to receive prayer. In the midst of this, I sensed the Lord telling me that He was about to heal cataracts. I invited all with that condition to come forward, and to my surprise at least a hundred people did so. Since there were too many for me to pray for individually, I asked them to place their hands over their eyes; then I prayed for healing. After only a few moments a great shout arose from them. I asked them to raise their hands if there eyesight had definitely been healed. I think that every hand went up. For an hour, people were being healed all over the field as the rain continued to pound down on us. Withered arms were made whole; deafness left. A woman testified that for a long time she had been unable to walk because of severe pain, but that now it was completely gone. At that point she began to run up and down the stairs to the platform while, once again, the crowd cheered enthusiastically. So much chronic pain left (with the people coming back the next night to testify and verify their healing) that it was impossible to chronicle it all.

• • •

and watched the special reports on television, the impact of actually being in Haiti was beyond what many of us imagined. Statistics, even photos simply did not convey what has happened to this nation. Every team member that I spoke with was greatly challenged and moved by what we experienced; yet all of them were thankful to have come during Haiti's great time of need. We gave and we received. We taught and we learned.

The only way we avoided being overwhelmed by the magnitude of the disaster was by learning to focus on the one person or family in front of us. Each had a story, either of loss or rescue. There is an indomitable will to the human spirit. In the midst of the countless tragedies surrounding them, these remarkable people kept moving forward, determined that tomorrow would a bit better than today. We encountered so much joy in the midst of suffering. One night I stood on the platform and watched as a thousand people sang and danced their jubilation and thankfulness to God. In the midst of such need, the smallest gesture of help was received with gratitude.

What has perhaps impacted me the most about our time in Carrefour is this—in 38 seconds, thousands of buildings were destroyed. Of the nearly 300,000 Haitians killed, over 100,000 of them were here in Carrefour. Everywhere I saw men and women with missing or destroyed limbs. Virtually everyone had lost loved ones. Yet in spite of this, I continued to meet joyful and thankful people. How could this be? In the churches, in the prayer meetings, at the outdoor gatherings there was the sound of rejoicing as people danced, sang and shouted their thankfulness to the Lord.

I joyfully added my voice to the chorus that I heard everywhere: "Merci, Jesu."

• • •

Recently, as I looked back over my notes, I came across something a friend wrote who had traveled with us on that first remarkable journey. He painted a picture with words, as only a poet can.

The rhythms of this country are so different from
my own. They permeate with the heat and dust,
or are transferred directly through outstretched
fingers of tentative children, who melt with a

*smile. Moments of contact breaking through
the frustration and weight of knowledge of the
separation between our worlds. We walk together
holding hands, feeling close. Briefly brother,
briefly sister. These children float butterfly-
like from one to another "blanc", seeking the
nectar that we also crave. Also seeking some
explanation for the loss, and it is great, both of us
wanting Papa to make it better.*

*But there will be no making it all go back to normal
after a brief embrace. It is not possible to undo
lives lost, to undo trauma seared into one's
dreams, without an undoing of the daily souvenirs
of the "tremblement de terre", when solid ground
is no longer solid and homes are no longer
shelter and refuge.*

*Je me souviens my children, (but not my children and
not my memories). Yes, they know the game – and
there might be some treat waiting at the end, but
there is a bigger hope that brings them to us. To
be seen, to be held, to be loved, to be assured that
it will all work out…*

16

ANOTHER JERICHO ROAD

The Good Samaritan might be Jesus' best-known story. Unfortunately, in our day it has lost much of its impact. Throughout the world, a Good Samaritan has come to mean a kind person, a good guy who helps someone out. The story that Jesus' first century Jewish audience heard, however, was both ironic and shocking. When Jesus talked about the priest and the Levite walking by on the other side of the road, His listeners must have smiled, knowing that the Jericho Road was only about 8 feet wide, making it virtually impossible for these two religious men to have simply not seen the injured man lying there.

But even more significant was the identity of the man who *did* stop to help. Samaritans were to be avoided by Jews at all costs. They were cultural and religious half-breeds, a people with strange customs and ideas about God. And this is where we in the 21st century lose the impact of the story. Perhaps if Jesus were to tell the story today, He would talk about the Good Muslim, someone with a different (and suspect) culture and strange ideas about God. But it was the Samaritan who represented the heart of the Father to the victim on the side of the road.

Some years ago, I came across a news article in a national magazine about two very interesting men in my city. After a second article appeared in our newspaper, I decided to hunt down these fellows. Chris and Paul were both HIV positive men who were giving themselves to helping the large population of men and women living on the streets in a notorious part of our city known as the Downtown Eastside. This area had the highest rate of HIV/AIDS infection and the lowest income in the nation. It was a community marked by violence, almost universal drug addiction, and despair. Chris and Paul worked on behalf of these people every day to gather food for a simple lunch, to connect individuals with support services, and to find shelter for these mainly homeless men and women.

After a short search—I had read that they worked in Blood Alley, which says a lot about the environment—I found them setting up a meal of day-old bread and pastries. I began to join them every Wednesday, bringing a case or two of fruit to pass out. This quickly became a highlight of my week. I would simply give out the food, and help with clean up while they were busy advocating for yet another vulnerable person. After a few weeks of this, Paul and Chris had a chat with me. During our talk, they discovered that I was a pastor, information that made them almost physically recoil

I began to join them every Wednesday, bringing a case or two of fruit to pass out. This quickly became a highlight of my week.

from me. Did I know that they were HIV positive? Sure. Did I know that they were a gay couple? I had figured that out. Then why was I, a pastor, coming down to help them each week? Because I could see how hard they were working and how valuable what they were doing was to the Downtown Eastside community, and if they were comfortable to have me, I would like to continue to help in my small way each week.

After a while, I found out that once a month, Paul and Chris put on a really nice meal at a local nightclub. They spent time gathering donations of food and finances from local businesses and restaurants so over 100 people from the homeless and HIV community could have a delicious sit-down meal. I went to help out in the kitchen. After most of the people had been served, Paul and Chris came into the kitchen to put together take-out meals that they took to the 10C ward at St. Paul's Hospital. In our city, 10C is the AIDS ward where people go to die. Like most people, I had heard of it, but had never been there. I asked if I could come along. What I experienced there marked me for life.

The first thing I noticed was there were no visitors. Secondly, there were no flowers or cards in the rooms. These men and women were alone during their last weeks and days of life. I followed Paul and Chris from room to room as they talked and gently joked with each patient. Often they would have to cradle these men and women in their arms in order to feed them because the patients were too weak to lift their heads. Many could only take a taste or two. For each person there was a kind word and a moment of complete attention as they were being loved.

To be honest, there was a backlash from some of my fellow believers; some of it came from a few in the congregation I led, some from fellow pastors. They were good people, but afraid of "Samaritans" who had wrong beliefs and wrong lifestyles. And perhaps, they were also afraid of the wounded left by on the side of the road at 10C—I had been afraid until I met two Samaritans who dared to stop, care and love. After all, isn't that the heart of the Father?

They were good people, but afraid of "Samaritans" who had wrong beliefs and wrong lifestyles.

> *"What do you think? Which of the three became a*
>   *neighbor to the man attacked by robbers?"*
> *"The one who treated him kindly," the religion*
>   *scholar responded.*
> *Jesus said, "Go and do the same." (Luke 10:26-37*
>   *The Message)*

17

FREEDOM FOR THE PRISONERS

I was shocked. In fact, I had Mike repeat his words, sure that I had misunderstood. Surely women were not put into a federal prison cell simply because they had sold goods on the roadside without a permit. Perhaps even more disconcerting was hearing that if these women had children five years of age or younger, they went into the cell too. Half of the children died from unsafe water and poor food. How could this be?

I had been travelling in five nations in Africa, building partner relationships and scouting for places where Impact Nations could come alongside and help. This was my first time in Nakuru, Kenya. I had just met a man who would become a good friend over the next few years. Mike, who I introduced a few stories ago, had been orphaned at eight years of age. For five years he had lived in the local garbage dump, surviving on scraps of food and selling bits of discarded metal. After that Mike lived in the city, part of a gang of thieves. One day he attended a crusade, intending to pick the pockets of the attendees. (Mike once told me, "If you can't pick the pocket of someone with his hands raised, then you can't pick pockets!") While at the crusade, his heart was deeply touched, and he turned to Christ. For over 25 years, God has used Mike to win thousands to Christ and to be a defender of the poor.

When Mike explained the situation with the women and children in prison, we put our heads together to see what could be done. None of the women had received less than a six month sentence; many were sentenced to two or more years. When it comes to justice, the Bible is very clear: God loves justice and hates injustice. The scriptures tell us this from cover to cover. So Mike persuaded the prison warden and the mayor to agree that, if the women's fines were paid, they and their children would be set free. I then posted the situation on our website and asked people to "click" to donate $88. This would pay a woman's fine, pay for a six-month work permit, and where needed, would provide for job re-training. As soon as this was posted on our site, immediately people from all over the world gave so that the women and children could be set free. These tangible expressions of active compassion touched me deeply—but more importantly, lives were literally rescued.

Only a few days later, photos of these women and children along with their stories were sent to us from Kenya. Because of the swift response from the West, the warden allowed us to post the pictures of another group of women prisoners and their children. Even more quickly, people gave generously and these women, too, were set free. Mike shared with me the joy of going into their cells (each woman and her children were kept in a separate cell), having the guard open the door, and saying to the confused, sometimes frightened women, "You're free! Someone on the other side of the world has paid your fine. It's true, you're free!"

Before long, we were able to free 32 women plus their children. As we continued to receive stories and photos from the women, we discovered that for some of them, liberation was bittersweet because their child had already died in the prison. In one testimony we received from a freed woman, we were told that when her one year old child died, leaving her with a three year old child still living in the prison, she had

"You're free! Someone on the other side of the world has paid your fine. It's true, you're free!"

come to such a point of despair that she began to plot how she could take her own life. She wrote it was then that Mike came and announced her freedom.

The experience of the powerful love of Christ profoundly affected all these women. There was no need to talk about God's love—He had broken into their lives and demonstrated His love. Although many of the women were Muslim, when they learned that it was because of their love for Jesus that strangers had paid for their freedom, all of the women gave their lives to Christ—even though we had made it clear that their liberation was unconditional and that nothing was expected in return.

In subsequent trips to Nakuru, I have often met women who were among those who were set free. I have been greeted with laughter, tears, kisses and hugs. I always tell them that it wasn't me, it was many people from around the world; but I get to be the recipient of their gratefulness. One grandmother, who had been freed while in the middle of an eight year sentence, ran to me and practically suffocated me in her rather abundant embrace. Today, she owns a used clothing business that provides for her six grandchildren and herself. Another of these women, less than two years after her release, had a successful career as a recording artist. Jesus really does make everything new.

Another of these women, less than two years after her release, had a successful career as a recording artist.

A year later, we were able to go back to the women's prison, where there were more ladies, again, many with their young children. I met some youngsters who were born in the prison and had never seen beyond its walls. I am grateful for two things that came out of that visit. Once again we were able to broker the release of another twenty women and their children. Secondly, we were able to install a water filter system that had an immediate impact on the health of the women and children. Whereas before half of the children died in prison, most of them from the effects of unsafe drinking water, since then, *not a single child has died*.

Like the disciples, I'm often a slow learner. For years, one of my favorite passages in the Gospels has been Luke 4:18-19. In this passage Jesus preaches His first sermon, announcing a whole new reality. Years ago, when I first read that He would bring recovery of sight to the blind, I assumed that He meant spiritual blindness, the kind that keeps people from seeing the truth. Then after a few years, I started watching as the blind *literally* saw. But even as I watched the blind receiving sight, I continued to think that "freedom for the prisoners" meant freedom for those who are bound up by their woundedness or in spiritual darkness. Now, finally, I think I've figured out what Jesus meant when He proclaimed freedom for the prisoners:

He meant freedom for the prisoners.

18

WHEN THE WALLS CAME DOWN

It has been said that no one feels neutral about India; people either love or hate this vast, teeming nation. For me, it was love at first sight (and sound and smell). I had become friends with a Hindu businessman in Vancouver, Canada. We often met for coffee and each time, Bill would say: "One day you must come to see my India." In 1997, that day arrived. I still remember the mixture of excitement and apprehension I felt while flying by myself to Delhi. I had been invited to minister at a church and at several house meetings. I enjoyed the ministry time and saw the Lord do some amazing miracles. But then after a week, the adventure really began.

My friend Bill flew over to meet me. He picked me up in Delhi with the greeting, "Now I'm going to show you the *real* India—*my* India." And that is exactly what he did. For about two weeks, accompanied by his brother-in-law Kewal and his nephew "Puppy", we traveled by car and train all over northern India. We stayed in villages, cities, towns and even ashrams—everywhere but hotels and other places typically frequented by tourists. And without exception, wherever we went, we were met with heartfelt hospitality.

Bill and I had become good friends in Vancouver, but for Kewal and Puppy, I was the first Christian they had met; their discomfort, and even nervousness, were apparent. And to be truthful, except for Bill's family, I had never known any other Hindus and so I am sure that I was also feeling less than completely comfortable. On the third day, all of that changed.

Weeks before, I had committed to preach at a church in Amritsar, a large city near the Pakistan border. Bill insisted that the three of them would accompany me, although none of them had ever been in a church before. As the four of us sat at the front of the church in the seats of honor, Kewal and Puppy looked rather frightened and decidedly uncomfortable. As far as I could see, they weren't actually shaking, but it was close.

After preaching, I invited the sick and injured to come forward for healing prayer. Immediately, I was inundated; and just as quickly, Jesus began to heal. I will always remember a woman being brought to the front of the church whose body was more twisted than any I had ever seen. As the Lord touched her, she began to shake. First her back straightened, then her legs and arms. Finally her incredibly twisted hands, wrists and fingers started to shake free. In a few moments, this young woman was completely healed. Nine hundred people shouted, clapped and sang. And all the while, Bill, Kewal and Puppy watched. The healings continued for an hour. Then, a very excited pastor asked the people to come and tell the congregation what the Lord had done. For almost another hour, person after person came forward with testimonies of healing; my Hindu friends seemed to be hanging on every word.

It had been a long day of ministry and travel, and I was bone weary. While driving back to the city, my friends decided to stop for supper at a roadside restaurant. Since leaving the church, they had been conversing non-stop, but of course I couldn't follow their Punjabi. While we were eating, I zoned out and didn't

For almost another hour, person after person came forward with testimonies of healing.

even try to join in the conversation. Then the restaurant owner came to our table and my friends began to talk with him—still I paid no attention. Frankly, all I wanted to do was get back to my bed. But all of a sudden, through the jumble of unfamiliar words, I heard Kewal say "Jesus". Suddenly, I was alert. Kewal was pointing to various parts of his body and telling the owner about all the healings he had seen that day. The owner then told him about the pain he always felt in his knees. To my amazement, Kewal, my new Hindu friend, said to the owner (Bill was translating for me), "Oh, Jesus will heal you!" Then Kewal turned to me and after telling me what the man needed, told me to pray for him. And Jesus healed the man.

For the next ten days, wherever we went, my Hindu friends told all who would listen about this Jesus who heals. Whether it was in a restaurant, a shop, someone's home, they would ask almost everyone they saw if they needed healing, then tell them that, for sure, Jesus would heal them. One evening we stopped overnight at a Hindu ashram. As soon as we got out of the car, Bill and Kewal began to call out until a small crowd gathered. They told the people about how Jesus had been healing everywhere we went. Soon, one after another pressed forward to receive healing. The four of us traveled together over 3,000 kilometers to cities, towns and villages all across northern India. And sure enough, Jesus did what He loves to do: He healed people of their sickness and pain. Not just Christian people. *All* people.

For the next ten days, wherever we went, my Hindu friends told all who would listen about this Jesus who heals.

During that unforgettable journey the Gospel got bigger, more flexible, more inclusive. And something else happened. While the Lord was healing hundreds of people in that church gathering in Amritsar, the hearts of four men also melted. Awkwardness and insecurity were transformed into comfortable affection, which in just a few short days grew into sincere love.

When I returned home to Vancouver, I began to get phone calls from people I had never met. There is an Indo-Canadian community of over 100,000 people in our city and the news of what Jesus had done in so many lives in India had already crossed halfway around the world. Every few days, another person would tell me what Jesus had done for a relative back in India, then they would ask if Jesus would heal *them* too.

Oh, yes.

19

INTO THE DARKNESS

And the light shines in the darkness, and
the darkness does not overcome it.

JOHN 1:5

A team from eight different nations was in Thailand for
two weeks. We were in the north, ministering to about 600
believers for several days. While much happened (including
a powerful outpouring of the Spirit that led to a revival that
went on for several months), one episode is etched in my
memory most clearly.

Thailand is a beautiful nation of remarkably gentle, loving
people. It is also a country that, especially since the Vietnam
War, has been held in the grip of prostitution and human
trafficking. It is difficult for us to understand how profoundly
this has affected the majority of the families. Young people
head to the cities to escape the grinding poverty that
permeates so many villages, and end up selling themselves
on the streets. Parents are approached by deceptive men and
women who promise good jobs for their children, either as

nannies or domestics. No matter what is promised, the result is the same—the children and young people are forced into the sex trade.

During one of the ministry sessions, a pastor from our team began to teach about the Father's heart. As he continued to speak, another member sensed that the Lord wanted to heal the heart wounds of fathers, mothers and daughters. At this point, we were unaware of how pervasive the sex trade was in Thailand. Surely, this wouldn't be a major issue among Christians? How little we knew and understood. As we began to pray over the entire group, crying broke out all around the room. Soon hundreds were wailing and sobbing more pitifully than I had ever heard. Men and women collapsed on the floor, howling in deep, desperate pain. Others held on to us, seemingly for dear life. It was deeply distressing and overwhelming. There were so many of them and so few of us. We moved from person to person, but truthfully, we hardly knew what to do and it shook us. Without a doubt, in all my life, I have never experienced that much pain.

Without a doubt, in all my life, I have never experienced that much pain.

A few days later, our team flew into Pataya, the prostitution capital of Thailand, where over 30,000 young men and women work in the sex trade. As I walked the streets with the pain-filled cries of a few days earlier still ringing in my ears, I felt a deep sadness for these young people. At the same time, a great anger rose up in me at the sight of so many middle-aged white men who had come from all over North America and Europe on their selfish and abusive "vacations".

The spiritual climate enveloping the city was so oppressive its presence was almost physical in nature. We walked through downtown, passing by the seemingly endless brothels and bars, praying quietly for God to break through. Then we went up on the top of the mountain to a tourist lookout point. From there we began to intercede for Pataya; we were oblivious and unconcerned with what others were thinking as we cried out to God on behalf of the city and the many who were trapped within it. As we then walked back toward the bus, one of our team was almost run over by a very angry man on a motorcycle. Another person was suddenly overcome with a blinding headache. We realized that we were in a very real battle.

That afternoon we went to the city dump, where many people scavenged daily for anything they could sell in order to buy food. For the next hour we distributed meals and food packets, then prayed for all who wanted prayer. We were kept busy for a long time. One of the best ways to change the spiritual atmosphere in any place is to actively come in the opposite spirit. In a city built upon the selfishness of so many Western men, simply giving food, encouragement and comfort was powerful in pushing back darkness.

That evening we stepped into one of the great adventures of my life. Earlier that afternoon, we had rented a meeting room at an upscale hotel downtown, where we set up tables with plenty of food and beverages. We "passed the hat" among the team and then gave a very large stack of money to my wife Christina. She and a couple of the women on our team then headed to the bars, while the men went to the beach and the streets and invited the working women to come to the hotel. This was a very confusing situation. It was difficult for us to communicate why we were asking these women to come to the hotel with us. All we could do was laugh at ourselves and at the strange situation we found ourselves in!

Meanwhile, the ladies went into one of the bars with their wad of money. In Pataya, most of the bars are also brothels, where the women stand or sit in something like a corral, waiting to be picked by a customer. The going rate to take one of these ladies out was just $7. Placing the large stack of bills on the bar, Christina asked how many girls the money would buy. A couple of minutes later she was like the Pied Piper, leading a parade of about 30 women through downtown toward the hotel.

Placing the large stack of bills on the bar, Christina asked how many girls the money would buy.

My wife isn't shy—even in the face of a potentially perilous situation, especially when it comes to rescuing women, whether it is in Nicaragua, Kenya, Cambodia, Thailand, or anywhere else.

By the time we all met back at the meeting room, about 75 young ladies had gathered with us. After allowing lots of time for them to enjoy the food that was laid out, I began to speak about how God wasn't angry or disappointed with any of them; instead, He loved them deeply, just as they are and not as they should be—because after all, none of us is as we should be. I then offered to simply pray protection, healing and blessing for any who wanted prayer. Then we waited. And waited. They all sat there silently. Finally, one brave woman stood up and walked toward one of the team. That was all it took; in a moment all of us on the team were surrounded. Over thirty of the women received the Lord (three of them came off the streets that night and went into a recovery home). A number of them were healed. I remember watching as one young lady who had been born with her ankle turned completely sideways, so that she walked fully on the side of her foot, was healed. But more than anything, I remember the tears. Eventually almost all of the women came forward. And what did they want? To be held. Held in the wholesome, reassuring, healing way a father holds his child. When the night was over, I left with my shirt soaked with the tears of many, many women, as did most of the team—especially the men.

Pataya may be the darkest city I have ever visited. Darkness can be intimidating, often repellent. But, as I have written elsewhere, Jesus was never frightened by the darkness of people's lives. In fact, He ran into the darkness because He knew that He had the solution. How easy it is for me to avoid darkness, or even look at it accusingly. But that's the thing about darkness—it's dark. Sinners sin. My avoidance and accusation can keep me from following the One who, everyday and everywhere, comes to rescue and restore.

In a way that I will never forget, God broke into that hotel conference room with His healing, compassionate, fiery love. But for Him to break into that room, first someone had to run into the darkness of that brothel.

Did I say just how proud of my wife I really am?

20

THE UNEXPECTED WAY HE MOVES

It has often been said that God is full of surprises. I think those surprises come out of not only His great love, but His infinite creativity. He is the One who is always at work, weaving a tapestry that sometimes confuses, but ultimately amazes and delights us. And like all great art, the sum of the whole is always greater than its parts. God is always creating; that is why the universe is constantly expanding. How could a finite creation express an infinite Creator?

It seems to me that there is a rhythm to the creative movements of this compassionate, forgiving, joyful, righteous and resolutely loving God. This rhythm is marked by rescue, reconciliation and restoration. Throughout the cosmos, God is bringing everything together, completing it in His Son, reconciling all of creation to Himself (Ephesians 1:10; Colossians 1:20). These are magnificent truths that I can barely understand. However, I know this: whenever we find ourselves moving in His rescuing, reconciling, restoring rhythm, we step into an accelerated velocity of what He is doing that can take our breath away.

In a previous story (*Freedom for the Prisoners*), I wrote about getting some mothers and their young children freed from prison and supplied with the necessities to build a new life for themselves. I was appalled and motivated by the situation; all I was thinking about was getting those women and children free. But by working to rescue them, without even being aware of it, I had stepped into the rhythm of God's Kingdom, where more happens, and happens faster than we ever thought possible.

We can see this in the feeding of the 5,000, the only miracle that is recorded in all four Gospels. In Luke's account, it seems clear that Jesus took the bit of bread and some fish and gave this small portion to the disciples for *them* to distribute to the crowd. It was only as they gave away their small amount that the miracle of multiplication took place. Working to free the widows and their children was similar to this miracle. We didn't have much; we weren't seeking to do more than something on a limited scale, but God took the little we supplied and multiplied it.

•   •   •

It was the day after Christmas, about seven months after we had been able to get the women and children released. On the other end of the line was Mike, my very excited Kenyan friend. He kept laughing and shouting into the phone, "You're not going to believe it! It's a miracle!" After a minute or two, he was able to tell me what had happened the day before in the men's maximum-security prison in Nakuru, Kenya.

Unknown to me, when we had worked to free the women

and their children, the atmosphere began to shift. There was both a growing awareness among the community, and an appreciation from the government, for what had been accomplished. Now, months later, Mike and his team had been invited into the men's prison to put on a Christmas feast for close to 3,000 men. This had never been done before. As part of their punishment, the prisoners were never given meat, surviving instead on mainly beans and corn. Imagine the joy as the team arrived with eight bulls that had been roasted for this feast. After the meal, they started to sing carols together. In the midst of the singing, the presence of the Lord came down onto that prison courtyard. The prison warden came over and said, "Mike, God is in this place." A few moments later, he looked intently at Mike and solemnly said, "It's Christmas. Mike, you and your team (who had been visiting as chaplains for some months) pick 200 men and today I will grant them an unconditional pardon." Among those pardoned that day were three men who were condemned to die.

That day, God re-wrote the stories of many men. One of them was Elly. When he was 16, Elly got into a fight with his friend. When Elly punched him, his friend fell, hit his head on a rock and was killed. Ever since that day, Elly had been in the prison. In all that time, no one had ever come to visit him. It was as though he had died with his friend. On that Christmas Day, Elly was set free. He was 62 years old. Not only was he freed, but Elly was invited to live with a family in Mike's church, where he continues to live to this day as a cherished member of the community. Psalm 68:6 declares: *He sets the lonely in families*. His final years have become

Elly's best years. Rescue, reconciliation and restoration. The rhythm of God.

This was a wonderful and totally surprising outcome, but God was still moving in the prisons.

Over the following months, we arranged for the release of more women and their children. When I took a multinational team to Kenya that spring, we were invited into the men's prison. After hearing from Mike about the previous Christmas, I was both curious and eager to see the prison for myself. Not surprisingly, it was a very oppressive place. The roughly 3,000 men spent their days out in the prison yard and every night in the cells. It was jarring to see a large set of cells marked "Condemned".

As soon as Mike's music team began to play, *everyone* pressed forward. I clearly remember Mike saying to the gathered men, "The only difference between you and us is that we didn't get caught." The men laughed and cheered, but there was much truth in his words. Several of our team spoke to the men and the Gospel was shared with them; many turned to Christ that afternoon.

"The only difference between you and us is that we didn't get caught."

But then it got even more interesting. A large metal tank had been brought in and filled with water. We were about to celebrate the prison's first ever baptism. I had no idea what big news this was. As the baptism began, there were reporters, microphones and cameras everywhere. A long line of prisoners formed beside the tank. In fact, 150 of the guards asked to be baptized as well. Several of our team moved up and down the lines, sharing Christ and leading the men in prayer. Before long, the water was the color of chocolate milk. And still they came. As we became tired, other team members would rotate in.   Others on the team prayed over each prisoner. After our allotted time in the prison ran out, Mike's team came back and continued baptizing. When we were finished, 680 men had come to Christ and had been baptized.

When we were finished, 680 men had come to Christ and had been baptized.

This story was carried on radio, television and newspaper, both nationally and throughout East Africa. For days, wherever we went, people would tell us that they had seen the baptism on television. On the following Monday, six young men from the prison were brought to court for sentencing. (They had asked members of our team to be praying for them.) When the judge asked the first young man if he had anything to say before sentencing, he replied clearly that he was guilty as charged, but that on Saturday, he had given his life to Jesus. The judge looked unimpressed—he had heard that story too many times before. But then the young man told him about the baptism. The judge replied that, indeed, he had seen that baptism happening on television. As a result, he gave the young man a suspended sentence. Immediately, the other five men charged told the judge (truthfully) that they too had been baptized. They received the same probation. A few days later, the president of the Kenyan national television called to tell us that the prison baptism was the most repeated news story ever covered during his tenure. The story ran for days.

And still God was moving forward.

The national media had been attracted because a baptism in a prison was something new. Their interest led directly to a national awareness of the prisons. Over the following two months I received letters from the head of the prisons and the vice president of Kenya, expressing both appreciation and telling me of how profoundly the prison had changed. In fact, my friend was sent by the government to an East African summit on prisons so that he could share with other representatives the profound impact of the baptisms. A year later, shortly before his term ended, the president of Kenya pardoned men and women who were being improperly held, either beyond the end of their sentence or because they had never actually come to trial. The number pardoned was an astonishing 6,000 men and women.

When we move in God's rhythm, there is amazing favor and acceleration.

When we move in God's rhythm, there is amazing favor and acceleration. Some of this we see unfolding, but much of what He does we never know. I will finish this with an entry from my journal, written three weeks after returning from our Journey to Kenya:

Just when I thought that all of the marvelous events and reports were becoming terrific (and empowering) memories— Mike once again surprised me. We were on the phone a few

*days ago and Mike told me that, again, Impact Nations had
been on national news in Kenya that day. Footage of medical
clinics was shown along with narrative about their impact
on the various communities. When I expressed surprise that
we were still news, Mike responded with: "That's not all.
You're not going to believe what happened."*

*The day when the Impact team was in the men's prison,
preaching to nearly 3,000 prisoners before the baptism,
unbeknownst to us, two ladies in the women's prison (located
just beyond the men's facility) were listening to us sharing
the Gospel. They knelt down on their side of the wall and
gave their lives to Jesus. They also prayed and asked Him to
rescue them from their upcoming sentencing hearing. Here
is their story:*

*Nine years earlier, their two boyfriends broke into a
house and robbed a couple, murdering them in the process.
One man disappeared; the other died four years later. The
police found some of the stolen items from the house inside
these two women's house. They were charged with murder
and convicted. For nine years they have been in the women's
prison, awaiting the sentencing hearing that they had been
informed would condemn them to death or life imprisonment.*

*Last week these two women were taken to the court for the
long awaited sentencing. The judge shocked them by telling
them that he was setting them free! After nine years with his
whereabouts unknown, the missing robber and murderer
suddenly turned himself in, saying his conscience would not
allow him to hide any longer. He also informed the court that
the women, in fact, had nothing to do with the robbery or*

murder. And so, to their utter amazement, the women were set free. This had made news everywhere.

While I had been preaching and as a forest of hands among the male prisoners went up, I knew that God was doing something very special. But as usual, He was working in ways that I had no idea about. If we will scatter the seed, He will bring forth a miraculous harvest.

Always, always God comes to seek and to save, to rescue, reconcile and restore. This is who He is; this is what He does; this is where He goes. And isn't it amazing—in all of this, He takes us by the hand and invites us to come with Him.

21

A TASTE OF HEAVEN

It is difficult to imagine a more beautiful place. We traveled through forests, passing through small hamlets where curious people came out to wave. As we climbed higher with each mile, the intense heat lessened. We headed further and further into the mountains that rose straight up from the Haitian seashore. It was a delight to the senses—the air carried the fragrance of tropical flowers; the hills were emerald green; everywhere were new sounds of unfamiliar birds. It seemed like a taste of heaven.

We had come to a mountain village that was little more than a loose collection of scattered homes—simple places with tin roofs and plywood walls. As we set up the mobile medical clinic, the first since we were here a year ago, the people began to come, all of them on foot. Most had walked a long way along the mountain road, really just a dirt track. Mothers carried children on their backs; the elderly came leaning on canes and walking sticks. We cleared a number of pews out of the church that we were using for the clinic to make more room. Before long, almost all the pews were outside, and still they came.

The church, high in the hills, was surrounded by even higher mountains. Some of the team pointed across the valley to a solitary figure etched against the horizon, high on the mountainside and miles away from us. Over the next couple of hours, we watched the progress of this elderly, solitary woman. Eventually she arrived, patiently waited for her turn, was treated and prayed for, then contentedly left the clinic to begin the long walk home. I don't remember her receiving any dramatic healing or miracle, yet her determination, patience and gratitude have stayed with me.

Our team had come not only with medicine, but also with water filters that would have an immediate and dramatic impact upon the health of the people. The biggest challenge was to find and get to the houses hidden among the mountains. A team of four set out in a jeep, for what I thought would be an hour or two. Seven hours later, they returned tired and very happy. After driving as far as they could before the track petered out, they began walking, carrying the filters and buckets. Unsure of where to go, they were delighted to encounter a young girl who happily took them further up the mountain to various houses—all of which needed access to safe drinking water. Each family was happy to share their filter system with their neighbors. When our small team finally returned, they told of healings, prayers and salvations. But what impressed them the most was how this small, scattered community of families truly cared and watched out for each other.

Meanwhile, the medical clinic continued hour after hour. Two or three hundred people received medical attention; each

What impressed them the most was how this small, scattered community of families truly cared and watched out for each other.

one was also offered prayer, which they eagerly accepted. As we see all over the world, the Lord graciously reached down and healed many. Pain and fevers left, deaf ears opened, cataracts dissolved and blind eyes regained sight.

As the reality and power of heaven broke in among us, many opened their hearts to receive Jesus.

While the clinic continued, others on the team walked up the road, offering prayer to everyone they encountered. They returned with numerous stories of healing and salvation. As they were walking back to the clinic, they saw an older man leading a donkey along the road. Someone asked the man if he needed healing; he answered that he was well. Then one of the women asked him if he knew Jesus; "No", he answered. When she asked if he would like to know Him, the man's answer was unforgettable. "I have been waiting for years for someone to tell me about Jesus and how I can know Him." To our western ears, that answer seems almost beyond belief, but that is precisely what the old man said. A few minutes later, he joyfully gave his life to the One he had been waiting to know for so long.

I have often found myself thinking about those three people: an old lady who doggedly walked for miles and miles to receive the only opportunity she had for medical care; a young girl who willingly led our team further and further up the mountain so that families could have safe water; and an old man who had been waiting quietly and hopefully for someone to one day tell him about Jesus. I think God was teaching us many lessons that day up among those beautiful hills. It seems to me the simplest lesson was that God's grace is everywhere, waiting to be both given and received, often in the most isolated and unlikely places. And whenever and wherever we recognize and respond to His quiet voice and His gentle leading, a bit of heaven breaks in.

"I have been waiting for years for someone to tell me about Jesus and how I can know Him."

22

FURTHER UP, FURTHER IN

Over the years, I have had the privilege of leading teams
on many exciting and deeply satisfying trips to some of the
poorest countries on the planet. But for sheer adventure, I
think that our journey to the city of Butuan in the Philippines
likely tops the list. It began with an invitation from the
Catholic Bishop for us to come and re-trace a journey made
over 150 years ago by an evangelist who traveled up the
Agusan River. He was the first person to introduce the native
people to the Gospel, teaching them God's truth through
song. For many years after, the sound of the village people
singing the Gospel to one another across the river could be
heard by travelers. Now, Bishop Dee Dee was asking us to go
back to these villages, some of which had not been visited by
outsiders in many decades.

When I had worked with the bishop on a previous
occasion, two things struck me about this remarkable man:
his love for Jesus was evident in everything he said, and his
commitment to unity within the church. I have never known
a leader more committed to church unity. For several years
he had succeeded in bringing together church leaders from

almost every denomination, both Catholic and Protestant, for a weekly prayer meeting for the city of Butuan. More than once I heard Bishop Dee Dee say in public gatherings, "There is only one church." Each time I ministered in Butuan, there was a powerful presence of the Lord and we saw many people come to Jesus. *When brothers live in unity, there the LORD bestows His blessing—life forevermore* (Psalms 133: 3).

This trip had another first—each day as we journeyed by road and boat, we were accompanied by members of the Philippine army. I don't mean three or four soldiers; no, we had about 100 soldiers traveling with us and another 200 stationed along the route. The soldiers were heavily armed and accompanied by an armored vehicle with

...each day as we journeyed by road and boat, we were accompanied by members of the Philippine army.

a large cannon mounted on it. As we bounced along some of the roughest and muddiest roads on which I have ever been, I was very aware that the cannon was pointing in the direction of the last army truck in the column—which happened to be the one in which I was traveling! The General explained to me that the bishop had insisted on this protection because we were traveling into an area filled with militant rebel groups. At one point, while heading to the first town, our team was stopped and re-routed because an armed skirmish had broken out a mile ahead of us. No wonder we were the first outsiders in many years to come to this area.

With this sudden change of plans, we found ourselves

entering a town where we were not expected. The Lord had changed our route because He had great things in store for us all. By the time we had set up the mobile clinic, there were already several hundred villagers gathered. There was no pushing or anxiety, just a lot of smiling people, curious, and happy to wait patiently. From the moment the clinic opened, the Lord began to heal people. I assured the crowd that, even if the Lord healed them through prayer, they were all still welcome to come into the clinic to receive medicine. In spite of this, many who were healed didn't go into the clinic; instead, in their excitement, they went to tell their neighbors what Jesus had done for them.

Recently, I visited with a friend who had been on that remarkable journey. She reminded me of an amazing healing. In the lineup for the clinic, Katherine had encountered a woman with a cloth over her arm who was in obvious distress. When Katherine lifted the cloth, she was horrified to see a burn so severe that the skin had actually been consumed, exposing muscle. She prayed fervently that the woman's pain would leave and the wound would be healed. Then she moved on. Some time later, Katherine went looking for the woman to see how she was doing, but was unsuccessful in finding her. She asked the medical team if they remembered seeing this particular woman. When they said yes, Katherine asked about the condition of the woman's arm. The medical team related to Katherine how this woman had approached them—crying—not with tears of pain, but with tears of joy. For some reason, she had kept the cloth over her arm while standing in line. When the nurse removed it, there was no wound or even a scar. Her skin was perfect; she had no pain. Jesus had done a healing miracle as the woman stood in the lineup.

While the team was fully engaged with the clinic, I took a translator and walked along the street, intending to ask people if I could pray for them; however, I only got to one house that morning. This was a small home with a dirt floor and almost no windows. The family brought me to their grandmother and explained to me that she was deaf, blind, and suffering from intense pain in her body. After assuring them that Jesus was delighted to heal their Lola (the Filipino name of respect for a grandmother), I began to pray. First, the pain left her body; then the Lord opened her ears. By this time, I noticed that a small group of teenaged girls had gathered in the open doorway, watching what was happening. A minute later, Jesus opened Lola's eyes. What I saw on the family's faces first was astonishment, then great joy. Jesus delights to heal; to restore wholeness to people's lives.

Jesus delights to heal; to restore wholeness to people's lives.

When I went outside the house, there was a group of about 25 teens standing in front of the house. This seemed like a good opportunity to tell them about Jesus. But as I spoke, I could tell my words were not having an impact. When I asked if any wanted to invite Jesus into their lives, there was no response. By now the gathering had increased to about 40 teens. Suddenly I remembered what Jesus had said in John's Gospel: *If you can't believe Me, then believe the miracles because they point to Me*. (John 10:38; 14:11) I asked this somewhat skeptical group: "How many of you know Lola?" They all did. (After all, we were in a small town.) "How many of you know that she can't see or hear?" "Of course", they replied. I then had someone go into the house and bring Lola outside where they could witness her healing. I explained to them that it was Jesus who had healed her. Now there was a completely different atmosphere; instantly, doubt had been replaced by faith. Within a short time, every one of those teenagers had given their lives to Christ.

•   •   •

Long ago, the Apostle Paul came to a town called Corinth. Looking back on that experience, he wrote:

Rather than using clever and persuasive speeches, I relied only on the power of the Holy Spirit. I did this so you would trust not in human wisdom but in the power of God. (1 Cor. 2:4-5)

What Paul understood, I learned for myself that day. Rather than being persuaded by my words, the Lord arranged for those young people to be established, from their first encounter with Him, in the reality and power of His Kingdom.

And so, this remarkable journey began. For the next ten days, the Lord took us further and further up the river—further from the security of the known, and further into His power and presence.

23

HOW FAR TO GO?

It was a week like no other. Each morning the team left while it was still dark, sometimes as early as 4:45; each night we returned about 10 o'clock. As tired as we were, there were no complaints. All of us knew that we were part of something unique, perhaps even historic. Every day as we went further up the Agusan River, which flowed through the island of Mindanao in the Philippines, we brought medical care to villages, many of which had never had a medical clinic. We traveled for hours along roads that were often so muddy they were more like bogs. And always as we traveled, we were accompanied by the detachment of soldiers.

The old expression, "Getting there is half the fun", never rang more true. We encountered unique challenges each day. On one occasion, one of our army trucks bogged down to its axles and was only extricated when a long, heavy cable was winched to a tree. Another day, one of the trucks (full of our team) began to list as one side sank in the mud. As it leaned further and further, the soldiers all jumped out and shouted for our team to do the same. The truck was close to tipping over and falling into a lake 40 feet below. While everyone else ran, one of the team stayed in the truck as it leaned precariously. Later, when I asked him why he didn't jump, he said that it was obvious: he didn't want to get his clothes muddy! Another night as we were returning from a village, I rested my feet on what I thought was some gear stashed in the army truck. I heard strange noises, but ignored them. Suddenly the "gear" moved. I discovered that we were sharing the truck with a pig!

While heading into one of the river villages, the General informed me that the authorities had kept written records of village activity for 150 years, and in all that time, no one had ever come with medical care. We were about to experience once again that God's sovereign timing is remarkable. I am sure that if we had eyes to see what He is always doing, we would be astounded. In this instance, we had a surgeon on our team for the first time ever. Five minutes before we arrived, a young boy had nearly cut his thumb off with a machete while hacking coconuts. We quickly set up a table as a surgical center and the surgeon repaired the thumb, using frequent shots of Novocain from the dentist's supply as pain relief. The surgeon later told me that if we had not arrived right then, this young boy would have bled to death. On that same day, a woman who was seven months pregnant was brought to the clinic extremely septic; untreated, she and her baby would die. The team was able to initiate care for her in the village, bring her back to

I am sure that if we had eyes to see what He is always doing, we would be astounded.

Butuan and have her admitted into the city hospital. In 150 years no medical team had ever come to this village, then on the very day we came, three lives were rescued. Only the Lord could have arranged that.

   "The LORD is good, a refuge in times of trouble"
      (Nahum 1:7).

It seemed like the whole village turned out that day, and why not? This was something completely new for them. There was a great atmosphere of celebration. Besides the medical care, many people were supernaturally healed. I remember walking by a tent where about 75 people were waiting to receive their prescriptions. I overheard one of our team telling them about the love of Jesus. I stopped and watched as every hand went up to receive the Lord as the invitation was given. When the clinic was over, although tired and facing many hours of travel back to the city, we couldn't get away as the village surrounded us *en masse* to express their gratitude. They sang, gave spontaneous speeches, and held on to us. What a wonderful time we had! This is the Kingdom. No wonder the 72 disciples returned from their ministry trip filled with joy (Luke 10:17).

   On our final day, we traveled five hours each way in order to reach one of the most isolated communities I have ever visited. We traveled for three hours in the army trucks, then another two hours by riverboat. This was a unique boat. It held about forty people, but was only wide enough for three to sit side by side, and the gunwales were inches above the surface of the river. The boat moved with a strange, rolling motion. Part way along our journey, one of the Filipinos told us to be on the lookout for a huge crocodile, reported to be in this part of the river. We all laughed (somewhat nervously), thinking that it was one of those local tales meant to scare tourists. Two or three months after we returned home, a news story was broadcast worldwide. It was a picture of the biggest crocodile ever found anywhere. And where was it captured?—exactly where we had been traveling. Nervous laughter, indeed.

At last we arrived at this isolated village. We climbed thirty feet up the riverbank to a tiny village where every house was perched on stilts twelve feet or so high. During the three month rainy season, the river spills its banks and the ground under the houses is covered by eight feet of water. During this season, the only way to leave your house is by canoe. The word had gone out about the clinic and so people paddled to the village from up and down the river. We saw a lot of dugout canoes that day because there are no roads in or out of this hamlet of 150 people. We set up our clinic under one of the houses to protect us from the tropical sun. This clinic was uniquely touched by God. There were far fewer people than on the other days, but as our team prayed for the sick and those in pain, the Lord healed one person after another. It went on for hours. As we later compared our experiences among the team, it seemed that everyone who was prayed for had been miraculously healed. And to our great surprise, once they were healed most of those who had traveled so far by canoe in order to attend the clinic got back in their canoes without seeing the medical team. Even though we encouraged them, even though we explained that the doctors were available right away, they just smiled and thanked us for praying.

It is interesting that we journeyed the furthest in order to go to the smallest community; after all, we had to travel for 10 hours—and not just us, but the soldiers as well. Was that a good use of resources? Wouldn't we have seen many more people if we had stayed in the city? But then I think about Jesus. He was always willing to stop for just one person. He reminds me that a good shepherd is willing to be impractical, to leave the flock in order to go after one isolated sheep. Jesus never seems to weigh the importance of things the way I do.

Jesus never seems to weigh the importance of things the way I do.

And that's my continual challenge in following Him—so often He doesn't go where I would go or do things the way I would do. It is so easy for me to march ahead, inviting Jesus to come along. But after all, He is the one who invited me to let everything be changed when He said: Follow Me.

Keep reminding me Jesus: *You lead, I follow.*

24

MORE THAN I IMAGINED

We were about half way through a twelve day Journey of Compassion to Uganda, our first time in that country. Western Uganda is beautiful; the hills are emerald green, like Ireland. This is a fertile land with rich, red soil that yields two harvests a year. And yet, the people here live amidst a grinding poverty that most of us can hardly imagine. Terrible roads that prevent crops getting to market, flash floods and increasingly unpredictable weather patterns that mystify the farmers, and corruption that paralyzes the economy—all of these belie the prosperity that should be Uganda's.

As we were about to enter Bulera, the next village on our busy itinerary, the Lord suddenly seemed to say to me, "Pay attention. This is the place." There was no doubt what He meant, and immediately my senses were heightened. I had come to Uganda with an awareness that Impact Nations was to give itself in a particular way to a community; the challenge was that I had no idea which one. Now, before I had met anyone in this town, or even set foot in it, I knew which place He had prepared for us.

Frankly, it didn't look poorer or in greater need than the

other towns we had been working in. However, part way through the day, two of our medical team, who had traveled with me to many nations, came and told me that the children in Bulera were the sickest we had ever encountered anywhere. "Are you sure? What about the kids living in the dump in Manila?" They insisted that these children were far sicker.

The Lord suddenly seemed to say to me, "Pay attention. This is the place."

Many of the children were suffering from acute malnutrition. They had all the signs—very thin limbs, bloated stomachs, orange hair, and most of all, these children were so *small*.

I began to ask the local pastor and headmaster of the school, Hannington, about current conditions. He showed me their water source which was only slightly better than a cesspool. This is where the children went to fetch water. He also explained that many of the children only ate the one meal a day that the school provided—about six ounces of corn mush—which was all that he could manage. With no protein whatsoever in their diet, no wonder the children were so small. The school met in the church building, a wooden structure with no windows and no electricity. Most of the light that came in did so through cracks in the planks. I saw children sitting as close to the walls as possible so they would have light to do their studies.

By the end of the day, I was trying not to feel overwhelmed. Where to start? Over the next few days, we came up with a simple strategy. We weren't really aware of it, but this strategy would become the prototype for the community transformation plan that Impact Nations would utilize in the ensuing years.

We determined the most immediate need in Bulera, after setting up water tanks and filtration systems, was to improve the children's nutritional health. To facilitate this, we began a program of encouraging all those who followed us on the Internet to fast one meal a week and donate what would have been spent on that meal toward our Isaiah 58 program. This money was used to provide a daily nutritious meal for the 150 children in the Bulera school. (This program has continued, and has been expanding, for over five years now, providing several hundreds of thousands of meals for hungry children in various nations.) Over the next few months, we purchased a few acres of land and provided the seed, fertilizer and herbicide necessary to grow enough crops to feed the children in a sustainable way. Eventually we built a storehouse and drying sheds for the crops.

It seemed that the second immediate need was electric lights in the school so that the children could study. There was a power line a short distance away, so we obtained a permit and arranged for an electrician to come from the city. A pole was put in the ground; the power line was extended to the school; and lights and fixtures were installed. Finally, the day came for the lights to be turned on. Now the children had enough light to read. At the same time, Hannington immediately began an afterschool program that extended into each evening. Besides helping the children to progress academically, Hannington had an ulterior motive. The children who would normally be at home in the evenings and therefore vulnerable to physical harm from drunken fathers, now stayed at school. He reported to me that by the time they went home, most of the fathers were in the bars.

We had simply tried to address a problem of not enough light for the children to read, but the Lord had something much bigger in mind. Shortly afterwards, Hannington called me with an amazing report. On the first Sunday morning after the power had been turned on,

We had simply tried to address a problem of not enough light for the children to read, but the Lord had something much bigger in mind.

many of the townsfolk showed up at church to see the lights. In the midst of the worship, the presence of the Lord filled the church. Almost every person fell to the floor, even though many had never been to the church before. They stayed on the ground until four in the afternoon! And when they got up, many had been healed right where they lay. So Hannington preached the Gospel and there was a great turning to Jesus. The following week, more people came from further away. After just three weeks, people were walking to the church from other towns and villages. The young people began to go door to door in the town, praying for the sick and telling people about what the Lord was doing in Bulera. Every week people came to Christ. And now, years later, it hasn't stopped. Three times the building has been expanded. We continue to hear ongoing reports of miraculous healings.

Since then, the school population has tripled. More farmland is being cultivated to feed these children. By installing the water tanks and filters, the children now drink clean water. The church continues to grow. A community is changing.

And all I saw was a need for some electric lights, clean water and one healthy meal a day. Each seemed like a great challenge. But the Lord saw so much more than I could see. Once again, Paul's words were proven true: *"Him who is able to do immeasurably more than all we ask or imagine, according to His power"* (Ephesians 3:20). I suppose that is why He told me, "Pay attention. This is the place."

It certainly is.

25

TODAY, SALVATION HAS COME

"I was in prison and you visited Me." MATTHEW 25:36

Over the past few years, with a growing awareness of God's heart for the prisoners of the world, we have taken teams into maximum security prisons in four nations—Kenya, Nicaragua, the Philippines and Haiti—as well as into women's prisons, and one children's prison in India. Why do we go to prisons around the developing world? God makes it very clear that He is in the business of bringing comfort to those who mourn and reaching out to the isolated, whether in the Beatitudes (Matthew 5:4), in Paul's second letter to the Corinthians (2 Corinthians 1:3-5), or in multiple places in Isaiah, Jeremiah and the minor prophets. If we will truly follow Him, Jesus expects us to be where He is, including in maximum security prisons. This journey has both surprised us with sublime moments of joy, and challenged us with times of great pain and frustration. I have seen prisoners fully pardoned, and I have talked with men who have been languishing for years in unspeakable conditions, without ever being granted a trial.

•   •   •

Good stories have a strong and happy ending; this one doesn't. But, as short as it is, this story needs to be told. Psalms 9 and 10 tell us clearly that God hates injustice. As His people, we must stand up on behalf of those who are powerless to defend themselves. And this begins with awareness.

When our Indian partners informed me that our team would be ministering to children in a prison, I was sure that I had misunderstood; but no, we were going to a prison for boys ages three to eighteen. When a child living on the street is caught stealing a piece of fruit or bread, he is taken to a prison with sixteen-foot high walls and a guard station. Others are picked up simply because they are vagrant. Other boys are dropped off at the front gate by parents who no longer are able, or want to feed their children. Most of the children I met there could not remember what was on the outside of the walls. Being there that day was a strange, almost eerie experience. We encountered boys who were excited to see us and, like boys everywhere, wanted to show-off and make us laugh. But even as we played with them, we knew that for many, they would never see the outside world. Instead, at eighteen they would be shipped to a men's prison. I am not making this up. This is real and it is happening right now.

Two of the boys had prepared a magic show for us and

other boys. As we laughed and clapped in delight, it was easy to forget for a moment where we were. The boys had

This is real and it is happening right now.

prepared skits and songs for us, as we had for them. We had a wonderful time telling them stories about Jesus as they listened intently. This amazing two hour time finished with our team praying for each of the boys. As we

left, I never imagined that it would be the last time we would see them. Some of the team had taken photos of all the fun; but then, back at the hotel, they posted them on social media. One of the prison authorities saw the pictures and our Indian partners were informed that, effective immediately, there would be no more visits to the children's prison permitted. Sadly, not every story has a happy ending.

• • •

We went into the maximum security prison in Chinandega, Nicaragua, with some apprehension. A few months earlier this prison had experienced another riot; there had been several over the past few years. The men were packed into cells that had been constructed for less than half as many prisoners. Not everyone had a bed; the barred windows were small and very high up; as a result, the men could not see out. As always, the guards were armed, but these guards seemed to be particularly tense and on alert. We had previously arranged for the men to be let out into the exercise yard where we had planned to both entertain them with songs and skits, and to present the Gospel to them. Before this, however, we fed all 1,100 prisoners a hot and nutritious meal that our Nicaraguan partners had spent many hours preparing. Even as we stood ladling out the food, the guards stood close beside us, reminding us not to get too close to the prisoners.

After the meal, we headed out to the exercise yard, expecting to see the men join us; however, at the last minute we were informed that it was not safe. Therefore, almost all of the prisoners had to listen from inside their crowded cells on the other side of the exercise yard. Disappointed, we nevertheless went ahead with what we had planned. After several songs, I asked my Nicaraguan friend, Osvaldo, to preach over the loudspeaker. Even though we could understand very little of what Osvaldo said, we were soon aware of the strong presence of the Lord. Through a translator I found out that Osvaldo was telling the men of his time as a young man in prison, and how the Lord intervened in his life. He then invited them to pray with him to receive Jesus. After prayer, he said, "I know you can't see me and I can't see you, but if you have just invited Jesus into your life, lift your hand up, right there in the cell. I can't see you, but Jesus can."

Throughout my many years of travel around the developing world, there are a few scenes that stand out, like snapshots, images that never fade. What I saw next was one of those images. As we looked across the exercise yard, all over the prison we saw hands waving through the bars of the cell windows. Somehow men had climbed up, perhaps being lifted by cellmates. In every window there were hands stretched to heaven. Hundreds of hands. I recall no cheering or clapping, but rather silence. It was a holy moment.

• • •

We were in the Philippines and our visit to the prison had not started well. Experience has taught us (often, painfully) that cross-cultural situations are always vulnerable to miscommunication, and that is exactly what had happened. For some reason, the prisoners had been told that we were coming to conduct a medical clinic. To this day, we have never figured out how they got that message. At any rate, when we explained that we had come to visit, to sing, and to tell them about Jesus, they were less than thrilled. We were informed that there had been no medical clinic for many months and that a lot of the men were sick or in pain. If only we had known, we could have helped, but we had no supplies or medical staff with us that day.

We set up a small sound system in a meeting room and waited to see if anyone would come. About 125 men decided that coming to hear us was better than staying in their cells. (The majority did not agree with them!) After a few songs and some healing testimonies of what the Lord had done that week, one of our team shared about his years in a Filipino prison in the north. He had the prisoners' full attention as he related his powerful story. Following that, I told them about what Jesus did for us all, and invited the men to open their hearts and lives to Him. I think about 50 of them responded. Then I told them that Jesus was about to heal the sick and invited any with pain to come forward. I still remember watching as eleven men shyly responded. I am certain that they were expecting me to pray for them, or the team that I had brought with me. However, I felt that I was to approach this situation differently.

I asked all those who had just moments before come to Christ, to please stand. Then I invited eleven of those prisoners to come and stand in front of each of the men who had come forward for healing. Now they looked confused, but eleven brave men came forward. Briefly, I explained to them that they now had the full Spirit of Christ living in them, and that knowing that truth changes everything. They did not need for His Spirit to grow in them; in other words, they didn't have to wait for a more mature believer to do ministry. Then, taking only a minute or two, I taught them a simple prayer model. After listening, they began to pray for their fellow prisoners. Soon hands were raised and voices got loud as the Lord used these brand new spiritual babies to bring healing. In a short time *all eleven men were healed*. Then more came forward, and they too were healed.

Before we left, I explained that Jesus had come to the prison and He had brought His Kingdom. The power of heaven was now fully available to them. From now on, when they were in pain or sick, instead of waiting months for a medical clinic to come, they could simply invite the Lord's healing presence to come, then command the sickness and pain to go. I told the men that what had been impossible yesterday was now possible today. Even the guards began to cheer. Some of them even came over and shook our hands; joyful prisoners hugged us.

As we left, I thought about what Jesus announced to the people of Jericho about a broken, outcast man: *"Today, salvation has come to this house"* (Luke 19:9).

26

JESUS AT THE MOSQUE

Over the past decade, I have had the joy of seeing many hundreds of Muslim men and women come to Jesus; in fact, it is likely well over a thousand now. Most of these men and women have been in India, Africa, and the Philippines. As a rule, when Muslims decide to give their lives to Jesus, they do so with a seriousness that comes from knowing that there will be a social and familial cost to their decision. I have also noticed how many of these men and women (especially the women) instinctively become effective disciple makers. On several occasions I have returned a year later to a village, only to be greeted by someone who first tells me that they came to Christ last year, then introduces me to the group of their friends and family that they have led to Jesus.

On many occasions we have conducted medical clinics in Muslim communities. This is usually a great surprise to them, until we explain that Christ's love and Kingdom are for everyone—no strings attached. Twice I have returned to one of these communities a year later and discovered to my delight that there was now a thriving community of Muslim followers of Jesus.

One such day stands out more than the others. On the previous Sunday, I had preached in a large church in Kenya. On that same morning, the Imam of the main mosque in the city was in attendance, on the invitation of the pastor. The Imam and I had a chance to speak for a few minutes afterwards and I even had the opportunity to pray with him. To my great surprise, a few days later, he contacted my friend Mike and asked if I would like to come to his mosque and preach. I could hardly believe what I was hearing. He also invited our Impact Nations team to attend. The only stipulation was that I was not to invite people to "become Christians". I gladly accepted.

He contacted my friend Mike and asked if I would like to come to his mosque and preach.

When we arrived, the Imam apologized that I would have to preach outside the front door, in the courtyard. He explained that there were a group of Somali men inside who had expressed their strong displeasure at my being invited to speak. I greatly appreciated the Imam's graciousness and courage; he could easily have canceled altogether. As it turned out, being at the front door was much better than being inside, because many more Muslim men and women were around to hear me. I spoke to them about Jesus, telling a few stories from the Gospels that revealed His great love for everyone, and His great power to change lives. Then I began to pray, inviting Him to come and touch us all. And He came. Immediately the courtyard was filled with both His peace and strong presence. When I was done praying, there was a deep silence. Just at that moment, one of our team went over to a woman and gave her a hug. To be honest, my first reaction was alarm; our team member didn't know it, but she had just done something that was never done in public. The Muslim lady began to cry softly. Immediately, more ladies on the team went over to the women. All over the courtyard, women were crying, clinging to Western women they did not even know. It was a powerful time.

Upon leaving the mosque, Mike said, "Now that you're finished preaching, I want to tell you something. One year ago this month, an American missionary stood right where you stood today. In one hand he held a Bible; in the other, a Koran. He then shouted out that only one of these books was the truth and that the other was a lie. He threw the Koran down on the ground. It was the last thing he did. In moments, the crowd had killed him." All I could do was thank my friend for not telling me that story sooner!

From there, we went downtown and preached Christ to a rapidly growing crowd; many came to Jesus. Then Mike and I sent the team back on the bus while I followed him into a secluded area of the main city park. There, we encountered about thirty young men. They were gaunt and sickly. They also each had a plastic bottle that they used throughout the day to sniff glue. While Mike talked to them about Jesus, he had one of his assistants run to a nearby store and buy enough bread for everyone. I think of what the Apostle James wrote:

> *"You see that his faith and his actions were working together, and his faith was made complete by what he did" (James 2:22).*

The Gospel was both proclaimed and demonstrated; this is a very potent combination. It proved so once again. *Every man there* prayed to receive Jesus and then gave up their glue sniffing bottles. I will always remember the sight of Mike coming into our hotel, calling the team together, then emptying two large bags filled with the bottles.

That night, Mike's phone began to ring incessantly with calls from those who had been at the mosque. We heard report after report of people being healed and coming to Jesus. Two men went home together and told their wives what they had heard about Jesus. God's presence came into their kitchen. Both of the wives opened up their hearts then and there to Jesus.

There is a postscript to this story. One year later, I returned to the same city where I met a young woman named Fatima. Unknown to me, while I was preaching by the front door of the mosque, Fatima was listening on the other side of the wall. When she heard about this Jesus who loves her right now, just the way she is, Fatima gave Him her life. Now, only one year later, Fatima and a small team are working every day in the various city high schools, teaching the students about Jesus. Remarkably, she

We can never know the impact of our words.

and her friends are discipling four thousand teens. She is also teaching new Muslim believers in her community.

We can never know the impact of our words. Romans 1:16 tells us that it is the Gospel itself (not our presentation) that is the power of God unto salvation. Jesus said that it is like a farmer who plants the seed and then goes away:

> *"Night and day, whether he sleeps or gets up, the
> seed sprouts and grows, though he does not know
> how. All by itself the soil produces grain" (Mark
> 4:27-28)*

How many times does Papa remind me not to worry about
the result? Just scatter the seed and let the "all by itself" life
that is in the seed do its work.

•   •   •

Recently I discovered yet another postscript to this
story. Following Mike's suggestion, I had brought along a
small laptop as a gift to the imam when I first met him. To
be honest, until Mike reminded me recently, I had forgotten
about the computer.

The imam was known as the foremost expert on the Koran
in the district, but he was curious to know more about Jesus.
And so secretly, using his new laptop, he downloaded the
Bible and began to read. One month later, the imam quietly
came to Mike and told him that he was convinced that Jesus
was the Son of God and Savior of the world. Mike prayed
with him and the Holy Spirit came upon this man powerfully.

About two years ago, the imam felt that he was being led
to a dominantly Muslim city in eastern Kenya, not far from the
Somali boarder. Besides leading the Muslim congregation, he
began a Sunday evening gathering for all those who wanted
to know more about Jesus. Before long, the group started

to grow; week after week, men and women were turning to Christ. Both congregations stayed relationally close. Instead of animosity, there was respect and openness.

In December of 2015, a news story was covered by the news media all over the world. A bus in eastern Kenya was attacked and stopped by radical Muslim terrorists from Somalia. They demanded that all the Christians be sent out of the bus to be shot. Instead, the Muslims on the bus told the terrorists that they would not send them out. If they wanted to kill the Christians, they would have to kill everyone. The terrorists were thrown into confusion by this and simply left. I remember the story well. What I didn't know until last month was that the people on that bus were the Muslims and the Christians that the imam from Nakuru was leading.

Once again I am confronted with both the intimacy and enormity of God's Greater Story. He always seems to take the little we give him and multiplies it beyond anything we imagined. In fact, much of the time we are not really imagining anything. The Apostle Paul said, *it is God who is at work in you, enabling you both to will and to work for his good pleasure*. (Ph. 2:13) God is always at work, weaving a tapestry of healing and restoration. He takes our little offerings of kindness, compassion, faith and love, and uses them as the threads to make something big and beautiful.

And now you know the rest of the story.

27

SURROUNDED BY GRACE

It had been a hard day. Our team was in a relocation camp in Haiti where hundreds of families had been stuck for nearly three years after the earthquake. We had been here once before, during their first year in the camp. At that time, there had been an atmosphere of optimism. Families had planted small gardens between the rows of tents; children's activities had been organized. I remember the council members telling me that they were determined that this would be the best camp in the nation. Now, two years of waiting for permanent homes had ground down their hope. The frustration and anger in the camp were palpable.

During the day we had conducted a mobile medical clinic. Instead of the joyful and thankful response that we were accustomed to in poor communities around the world, our team was met with a somberness, almost a resentment. We found ourselves repeatedly calming down volatile situations. At one point we even had to physically step into the middle of a fight that broke out. By the end of the clinic, the team was tired and somewhat stressed.

After supper, we went back and held an outdoor meeting

with music, testimonies and simple Gospel preaching. I remember feeling like I was talking to a stone wall. Then one of the teenagers on our team asked if she could share something. I quickly and quietly warned her not to be discouraged if the crowd didn't respond. As she spoke, it was as if ice was melting. With every sentence, the people became more and more responsive. An invitation was made to come to Christ and to my utter amazement, hands went up all over the field. When it was time to pray for the sick, there were so many crowded at the front that we couldn't get to them; I had the team move 50 yards away and invited the people to come to them. About 150 people walked across the dark field to receive prayer from the team.

Once again, Jesus reached out in compassion and power to heal. In the midst of it all, I particularly remember two healings that clearly expressed the heart of the Lord. I watched as two ladies from Canada prayed for a five year old girl who had been born completely deaf. They laid their hands on her ears and prayed. After a few moments the little girl's eyes suddenly got wide. Then she started looking all around. It was obvious that something was happening. When the people around her saw this, they began to cheer. This little girl covered her ears and began to cry. She was frightened with the entirely new experience of hearing. Once again, I was struck with the powerful truth that in a moment, not only had her ears been opened by Jesus, but the entire direction of her young life had instantly changed. The social, educational and vocational limitations that she was facing as a deaf person were now gone. A life rescued.

But then only 20 feet from where this little girl's life had been changed, an old woman approached me in the dark. She was moving very slowly, leaning on a crutch with an arm brace. When I asked what she needed Jesus to do for her, this lady told me that her back was very sore. After assuring her that Jesus was going to heal her back, I reached around to put my hand where she had indicated there was pain. To my great surprise, I suddenly realized that she had a huge hump on her back. She was more profoundly hunchbacked than anyone I had ever seen. I admit to an internal 'gulp' happening inside me as I placed my hand on the hump. By now there was a sizable crowd gathered around us. As I prayed, I felt the hump getting smaller. As it shrank, this lady began to progressively stand straighter. In only a minute or two, the hump was completely gone and she was standing up straight. She began to walk, feeling behind her for the hump that was no longer there. Suddenly, she threw her crutch away and began to walk back and forth, faster and faster. One neighbor shouted out to anyone who would listen, "I know this lady, and I'm telling you she was bent over and couldn't walk!" A great cheer went up from the crowd.

From time to time I think about these two healings, only a few feet apart. I see them as bookends of God's love and mercy. Over the years I have seen Jesus

"I know this lady, and I'm telling you she was bent over and couldn't walk!"

instantly heal a number of children born deaf. Every time, it touches me deeply to see how He reaches out and rescues a young life. But that night I saw another expression of just how wonderful and all encompassing are His mercy and grace. This grandmother was obviously in the final stages of her life, a life lived with the pain and stigma of being a hunchback and cripple. Yet Jesus didn't think she was too old. He didn't say, "Don't worry. Soon you will be with Me and then you will know perfect health." Instead, like the cripple at the pool of Bethesda who had suffered for 38 years, He reached out to this old woman and said, "Today is your day."

> *"The LORD, the LORD, the compassionate and gracious God, slow to anger, abounding in love and faithfulness." (Exodus 34:6)*

28

THREE LIVES

The past decade of working among some of the poorest people in the world has taught me something: Opportunity unlocks potential. It is all too easy for me to overlook the giftedness that God has placed into each man, woman and child. Poverty, illiteracy and sickness blind me to the person that is really there. But each person I meet is "fearfully and wonderfully made" by an infinitely creative and loving God.

The stories of the following three women intersected with mine; each of them opened my eyes a little more.

In India there are over thirty million widows. Many of these are young women, often not yet out of their teens. This is the product of a tradition whereby fathers essentially sell off their daughters as wives to much older men. When the husbands die, these women are immediately cast out of their home and usually the village as well, since widows are considered very bad luck. They are left with few options other than begging, prostitution, or suicide.

Several years ago, working with our partners in India, we established sewing schools where these women could learn a trade and thereby become self-supporting. Upon graduating from a six month sewing and small business course, each woman was presented with a sewing machine, and all the materials necessary to launch her business. Over four hundred women graduated from this program. Most went from being completely illiterate and unskilled, to becoming small business owners.

Ravathi was twelve years old when her father arranged her marriage to a much older man. She went to live with her unknown husband and his family. When she was fourteen, Ravathi had a baby. Immediately upon the child's birth, her husband's sister took the baby away and killed it, since the in-laws did not want another mouth to feed. A year later Ravathi was pregnant again. This time her in-laws forced her to have an abortion. One year after that her husband died. Ravathi was expelled from the home, but not before being told that her husband had been HIV positive, and now so too was she. Then, in the midst of her despair, everything changed. My Indian friends encountered Ravathi sleeping at the edge of a field and invited her to move to their home. She then entered the six-month sewing school program. Ravathi was a gifted seamstress and she also became, it turned out, a fine instructor. Arrangements were made for her to receive lifesaving anti-retroviral medicine; she remains strong and healthy today.

Jyote's story is similar. A mother of two, after her husband died, she was put out of the village. In despair, she tied her children around her waist with a rope and leapt into a well. But God had other plans for Jyote. Someone saw her jump and rescued her and the children. Like Ravathi, she was invited to live in a Christian home and was given the opportunity to learn how to sew. In the beginning, because throughout her life she had never been given any opportunity to go to school, Jyote knew very little and even had to be taught to read the numbers one to ten. Six months later, she graduated from the sewing school and began her own home business in another village. This formerly illiterate and untrained woman had great God-given gifts. Within a year, she had started her own sewing school in her home village. Shortly thereafter, Jyote made the journey to Hyderabad, a large city many hours away. There she met with the management of a major clothing company. As a result of this meeting, Jyote now has her own business that employs a number of women from her village and has a clothing contract in the city. All of that gifting and potential had been lying dormant for years, just waiting for an opportunity to flourish.

We encountered Jane over two years ago in the village of Kalonga in Uganda. Like so many women in that nation, Jane had, without warning, been abandoned by her husband and left to fend for herself with five young children. Rarely have I met anyone who looked so sad, so completely devoid of hope, as Jane. She had no place for herself her and the children. Constantly, she was being driven away by other villagers. When I first met her, she and the children were sitting desolate in the dirt. At night they huddled in a tiny dirt hovel—it could not even be called a hut—and in the daytime Jane did whatever work she could find, in order to get enough beans and corn for her children to have one meal. Some days she succeeded, some days she did not. Five months before meeting Jane, on the other side of the world, the Lord spoke to a few of us and said that we were to give ourselves to Kalonga. We went to Kalonga to scout out the situation, and that is when we came across Jane and her five children. I am convinced that Jane was in the center of God's heart when He sent us to Kalonga. We felt the Lord reach out to her as we prayed for her and her family. Since that day, He has opened many doors for us to help bring about transformation in this village. Just last week I was in Kalonga and once again saw Jane—although at first I didn't recognize her. Instead of a sad, broken women sitting in the dirt, I was standing before a smiling, beautiful, and finely dressed lady. What struck me so powerfully was her joy and her *confidence*. As we talked, I felt tears well up in my eyes. Given the opportunity, Jane was now flourishing. Her children were in school and she had a simple home with a plot of land that she owned. Furthermore Jane was in school, training to become a seamstress, with a job waiting for her upon graduation. She had made the most of each opportunity given to her.

I think I can usually tell where God is at work. It's the place where lives are being rescued, restored and reconciled. It is where the invisible ones become visible, where abandonment is defeated by the gift of welcome. After all, Jesus said, "Behold, I am making everything new!" (Revelation 21:5). That is what He does. New beginnings. New adventures. New opportunities. And as

It is where the invisible ones become visible, where abandonment is defeated by the gift of welcome.

always, He invites us to be a part of what He is doing; in fact, He usually seems to do His work *through* us. But I need to have eyes to see beyond what is, to what can be, because that is where God is—whether in India, Africa, or the town where I call home.

> *Man does not see what the LORD sees, for he sees*
> *what is visible, but the LORD sees the heart.*
> *(1 Samuel 16:7)*

29

BEHOLD, I MAKE EVERYTHING NEW

Go out quickly into the streets and alleys of
the town…   LUKE 14:21

My wife Christina travels to many nations each year, both with me and on her own. What often calls her away to foreign countries is the invitation to minister to women and children trapped in the sex trade. For many years, I have watched how the Lord uses Christina's passion and giftedness to bring hope and freedom to many. Here is a story, told in her own words, of how her willingness to "go into the streets and alleys" opened a powerful door of freedom for many.

In September of 2013, we were in Nakuru, Kenya with a Journey of Compassion team. One evening, we joined a few locals from our partner church there to reach out to the women "working" on the streets. Uneducated and without any kind of job training, these women have few opportunities to earn a living and are forced to sell themselves in order to feed their children. Their stories often relay how pimps offer to pay some bills or give free drugs and then force them to work off the repayment, thereby enslaving them.

We were told to expect about 20 to 25 women, and we had put together 23 small bags of toiletries to give away. Under normal circumstances the ladies would be taken to a coffee shop, bought a coffee for a visit and prayer. However, there had been a terrorist attack in Nairobi the previous week and our partners felt it was unsafe for our team to meet the women in a public space. Instead, it was decided we would have to congregate in an alleyway downtown. I love Steve's teaching that Jesus "ran into the darkness", so in spite of feeling apprehensive, I knew He was with us.

I trust God to keep me safe, however I admit it was rather daunting to lead the group of fifteen into that dark alleyway. A few locals headed out to let the women know where we were. I can still hear our prayers, asking God to bring in those who needed to receive His love, our voices tinged with some fear and apprehension. We stood under a dim streetlight, trying not to be overwhelmed with the smells and sights of our surroundings.

A uniformed policeman who attended the local church came along and told us it was unsafe to stand where passersby could see us. So moved us even further down the alleyway where it was pitch black! He then stayed at the opening to the alley, guarding against any danger.

The women began to gather, and as they did, we simply visited with them. It was so dark all we could see were the whites of their eyes and their beautiful smiles. Remembering that my friend, who left her life on the streets after many years, tells that her rescue started with someone smiling at her and treating her like she wasn't invisible, I knew the value of treating the women with dignity. I began to share some personal stories of experiences I'd had, including my friend's. God had rescued her, and her whole life had been transformed when she gave herself to Jesus and trusted him with her future. In fact, she herself is now an important part of rescuing others. Then other team members shared about being set free from drug addiction and relational brokenness. There, in a dark alley, late at night, the give and take of real life was happening as our team and the women exchanged stories and opened up hurting hearts both past and present.

One woman, who seemed to be a spokesperson, said, "We're not stupid, you know. We don't want this lifestyle. It's just that we don't have any other choices." Our hearts were troubled that they might think we were judging them, as so many have. How could we not think of the woman caught in adultery who was brought to Jesus? Our desire was that they could feel His compassion flowing through us.

I informed them that Pastor Mike had been helping many of the poor in the city to get entry-level jobs or to set them up in a small business. I also explained to the women about the opportunities, that help was available to them. We chatted some more and then offered to pray for them. As each one received prayer, tears flowed.

This was no momentary encounter; we were there close to two hours. I gave them information about the local church where they could receive ongoing care. We then offered them the small gift bags that we had brought. It was at this point we realized that there were 87 women gathered! We encouraged them to share what we had brought, which they gladly did, expressing delight as they lifted out each item. It was a privilege to know that we had touched all those lives with the love of Jesus.

The next day, Pastor Mike came to our hotel with two young women, one of whom was named Rose. He told us this story:

At nine o'clock that morning, 23 of the women we had ministered to the previous night had showed up at his church, looking for help in getting off the street. Mike and his team were prepared for them and immediately began to introduce them to job training opportunities. Our entire team rejoiced; what a wonderful outcome to our small efforts! Mike then explained why he had brought Rose to meet us. Rose, 13 years old, had come to the church with her mother who had been in the alley the previous night. A year earlier, her mother's pimp had forced her to bring Rose out onto the street and to begin to sell her body. As we looked at this beautiful young girl, it was hard for us to comprehend that she had been prostituted for a whole year. That morning, her mother came looking for hope. "Mike, will you help me? I don't want my daughter to have this lifestyle anymore. I want her to have a better life. Please, Mike, will you help me?"

With full agreement from both Rose and her mother, Mike took Rose to a home that his church has established for young women. The young woman who directs the home thanked us for rescuing Rose's life. After discussing it among our team, we gathered some clothes (she only had the clothes that she wore to attract men on the streets) and some money. We were able to pay for her education for a year—her school fees and uniform. This young girl who opened her heart to Jesus now lives a radically different life. Her possibilities have entirely changed; she now has a very different future ahead of her!

What a blessing to be a part of Rose's story. The Apostle John wrote that the light shines in the darkness, and the darkness does not overcome it. That promise is what takes us to ghettos and dark alleys. I love running into the darkness with Jesus.

30

A DIFFERENT KIND OF CHURCH MEETING

For more than 30 years, the early church has fascinated me. For three centuries, through persecution, slander and rejection, the church grew at an unprecedented rate without the benefit of public gatherings or buildings. For years, my reading has led me to an interest in the house church movement in China and India. A number of years ago, I heard about Victor Choudhrie and a movement that began in his home in the early 1990's. This movement now includes many millions of people all over India. The numbers are staggering: for each of the past three years they have celebrated Pentecost Sunday by baptizing *one million* new believers in towns and villages all over the nation. Hundreds of new house churches are being added every day.

In 2013, I flew halfway around the world to see for myself what was happening. In a three week time span, I traveled over 2,500 kilometers while there, visiting house churches in isolated villages, farms, city slums and modern neighborhoods. With impeccable timing, I was in India during the most severe heat wave in forty years; I remember

161

one day was 51C/124F. Yet even this didn't stop people from crowding into small rooms with little or no ventilation. God is moving powerfully and no one wants to miss out.

My friend Anuroop and I drove into a remote, rural area populated by the Banjara people. The Romany people (sometimes referred to as gypsies) originated from this region and descended from the Banjaras. Many centuries ago some of them emigrated to Persia and on to what is now eastern Europe. The Banjaras are an isolated, poor tribal people, largely ignored by the surrounding communities. We stayed overnight at a friend's home; the next morning people began to arrive from all over. After some time, there were 46 men, women and children packed into the small house. I was about to witness a new and totally different kind of home gathering.

I was about to witness a new and totally different kind of home gathering.

No one called the meeting to order, or even asked if someone had a scripture or prayer. Instead, the Holy Spirit led. Someone began to sing and others joined in. Then another person began a song that was picked up by all. Someone began to pray, then a scripture was read, then another song. For 2½ hours, there was a continual flow of testimonies, songs, prayers, scriptures and teaching—and all of this happening with no one directing in any way.

At one point, a young girl of about 13 years of age read a passage from 1 Samuel, then began to share with the church what the Lord had spoken to her through this passage. It

was a remarkably deep teaching, full of revelation. Another
person told an original parable about a factory manager and
his workers. A woman testified that earlier in the week, while
in prayer, the Holy Spirit told her that a certain man in the
village had died. She was directed to go to his house and,
rather than praying for the man, she was to preach the Gospel
over his corpse. She did exactly that. The man suddenly
began to breathe and then sat up. I was astounded, yet all
around me there seemed to be no surprise, just thanksgiving.
Someone else shared that she had had a wonderful week,
leading 22 of her neighbors to Christ. Then she baptized
them all at her home. Twenty-two neighbors in one week.
Another woman told of going to a home where a woman had
died. She laid hands on her and
prayed; Jesus brought the woman
back from the dead. Once again,
there was no surprise expressed
among the church members, only
thankfulness and joy.

*She laid hands on
her and prayed; Jesus
brought the woman
back from the dead.*

New believers shared their
stories of recently coming to Christ and of how excited they
were to tell all their neighbors about what Jesus had done.
Many testified of meeting the Lord through the kindness
of a stranger who later became a brother or sister. In this
incredible atmosphere of faith, love and victory, many of
those visiting for the first time also gave their lives to Jesus.

Finally, the host in this small Banjara home spoke. For the
whole time he had been simply watching and enjoying what
the Lord was doing. He said to those gathered, "Once again,

the Lord has richly blessed us. This has been a wonderful time. It is near the end of the month and I know that you have all been asking the Holy Spirit about how many disciples (i.e. new believers) you should be asking Him for over the next month. Let's take a few minutes and each one can tell what He has said to you." Without hesitation, all the believers spoke out a specific number. The lowest I heard that morning was five; the highest I remember was forty. One woman began to weep loudly. She told us that earlier in the year, she had asked the Lord for 300 new disciples this year. She had already surpassed that goal and it was only May. When she prayed, the Holy Spirit told her, "Daughter, why don't you ask me for 3,000?" It was this answer that had brought her to tears. She was convinced that the Lord would give these people to her.

Afterward, I thought of what the Apostle Paul told the Corinthians: when the church gathers, *each one* has something to contribute (1 Corinthians 14:26). As each person stepped out and shared, it was as though the Lord was weaving a tapestry that was different every time they gathered, but always made from the mutual love, joy and faith that each individual added. This is what I saw, and it was thrilling. The time flew by and I didn't want this gathering to ever end. No wonder the house churches keep multiplying all over the nation. Who wouldn't want to be in the midst of this?

This was my first Indian house church experience and it has had a profound impact on me. Later, I saw this repeated again and again as I traveled around India for the next three weeks. Each gathering was unique, but what tied them together was a great excitement and appreciation for what the Lord was doing, and a hunger among all the participants to continually reach their friends and neighbors with the amazing story of the Gospel.

At each gathering, time seemed to fly by; I felt like I had stepped into the book of Acts—and it was a great place to be. As a North American pastor, I had for years studied techniques, strategies and programs designed to help the church grow. But what I saw in India was organic; it had so much life that *it couldn't help but grow*. Just like the early church.

> *They broke bread in their homes and ate together with glad and sincere hearts, praising God and enjoying the favor of all the people. And the LORD added to their number daily those who were being saved. (Acts 2:46-7)*

31

LEARNING IN THE BATTLE

My first personal encounter with HIV/AIDS was when I met a young man in the early 1990's who said to me, "I would really like to come to your church, but I know I can't." Intrigued, I asked him why. He then explained to me that there where were two reasons I wouldn't allow him to attend the church. Although no longer practicing, he had lived for many years in the gay lifestyle. Secondly, and sadly, like so many others, he had also been infected with the AIDS virus. As we talked this through, I assured him that not only would he be welcome but that, being part of a supportive and committed community would be a great help to him in his battle with AIDS.

Over the next three years, Rick actively participated in our growing church community. His artistic and technical abilities were encouraged and given lots of room to grow. Admittedly, in the beginning, I wondered how he would be received into our church community. I found I had nothing to be concerned about as people consistently reached out to Rick, encouraging and including him in their lives. And then, as so often happened in the early days of AIDS, Rick's health began a sudden and rapid deterioration. Many times we prayed for his healing. We had started to see serious cancers instantly healed; yet Rick's health continued to decline. Then, one day, he died. His parents were understandably heartbroken; Rick was their only son, and he had been very close to them. I will always remember their unbridled grief as I officiated at Rick's funeral. I went home that day, heavy with the sadness of losing a friend, and deeply disappointed that, even though I had prayed earnestly with all that I knew, Rick had not been healed.

Three years later, I was pastoring a church on the other side of the country. It was there that I met Cheryl. She was a large, vibrant woman with one of the most exuberant laughs I had ever heard. Cheryl lived life fully—with joy, boundless enthusiasm and a great love for fun. Soon after joining our congregation, Cheryl's husband gave his life to Christ. He was a very large man; it was quite a sight to see Reg pulling a small red wagon along our downtown streets, carrying a large caldron of soup, which he lovingly ladled out to the homeless. This was something he did several times a month. One day, Cheryl came to see me; she informed me that she was HIV positive. Cheryl had been an AIDS specialist with the UN. One day, she helped another nurse to strip a bed; unknown to her there was a dirty needle in caught in the sheets, which pricked Cheryl's hand. Later tests confirmed the worst.

This came as quite a shock to me; she seemed so strong and healthy. A year later, Cheryl had all her friends over to celebrate her 40th birthday. She said it was a special celebration; ten years earlier, a doctor had told Cheryl she would never live to the age of see forty. However, less than two years later, the virus began to attack Cheryl's body with a vengeance. In less than a year, she lost over one hundred pounds. Still, her faith that the Lord would heal her never wavered. We were a close church family, and it seemed that every member took on the challenge of her healing very personally. There were days and weeks of fasting. There were corporate prayer meetings at the church; there were smaller gatherings, often at Cheryl's home. And always, she kept on believing, declaring again and again that AIDS was a mountain that we were going to climb and defeat. There were small miracles: her viral count went down, various positive counts went up and stayed up. She wasn't free of the virus, but it was clearly on the run; at the same time, our dear friendship became even stronger.

Then one weekend, Reg and Cheryl went camping and she caught a cold. The infection ravaged her body. By Tuesday, Cheryl was in intensive care at the hospital. By Thursday she was moving in and out of consciousness. Through all these days, I deeply interceded for her healing. On Saturday morning, Cheryl slipped away. The last thing that I remember her saying to me was, "Don't you quit. Don't you quit." I knew that she wasn't really talking about her own battle; Cheryl was telling me that if we kept pursuing this ministry of healing, one day we would

The last thing that I remember her saying to me was, "Don't you quit. Don't you quit."

see people healed of this terrible disease.

•   •   •

Four years later, I was leading a trip to Venezuela. One day, I found myself praying for a long line of people. As I stood in front of a woman, she told me that she had AIDS. (This is something that I had often encountered.) I prayed for her and then she told me with great confidence that she had felt the Lord do something in her body and that she was now healed. I told her, as I always do, to go to a doctor for confirmation. Then I moved on. Three days later, I was teaching a group of pastors in another city. In the middle of my teaching, one of the translators from the team burst into the room and, without waiting for me to stop teaching, shouted out, "She's healed! She's healed!" I was totally confused, having no idea what he was talking about. I found out that the woman that I had prayed for earlier in the week had just finished two days of various tests in the hospital. There was no trace of HIV/AIDS in her body.

Instantly, I heard Cheryl's voice, "Don't you quit. Don't you quit." With tears in my eyes, I said right back to her, "We got one, Cheryl." Since then, we have begun to see a trickle of such healings. My wife prayed for a woman in Kenya who, after prayer, had two days of testing done. She, too was completely healed. I shared this story with a friend who has a church in Uganda. Some months later when he prayed for a girl with AIDS, she too was totally healed.

We haven't finished climbing that mountain yet, but we are well on the way. We are in a war. If ever we are unsure of that, all we need to do is to step into the frontlines of sickness and oppression. Here the nature of the war becomes clear. Like all wars, this one will be won battle by battle, not all at once. We don't win all the battles. This is why Jesus, in the book of Revelation, so often declared that in order to take hold of our inheritance, we must learn to be overcomers. Learning to live in this reality is a hard, often painful journey. It is filled with uncertainty, disappointment and confusion. But Jesus also fills this journey with hope, joy, and wonderful surprises. Through it all, Jesus keeps telling us, "Don't you quit."

"The reason the Son of God appeared was to destroy the devil's work." (1 John 3:8)

32

WE WALK BY FAITH

As we drew near the close of our Journey of Compassion to Jacmel, Haiti, I was aware of feeling a growing apprehension over what awaited me. Instead of returning to Canada immediately, I had committed to visiting the mountain community of Bouvier. Beginning in the early 1800's, Haiti has had a history of violent and deadly uprisings, resulting in many evacuations to the safety of the remote mountains that make up most of the country. Apart from being a place in which to escape, there are no discernable reasons for why Bouvier exists in this location. There is no water source—people have to walk about three-and-a-half hours each time they need water. The steeply sloped land is very poor for growing crops, other than small vegetable plots. There are no shops; everything must be carried up the mountain trail without the benefit of a vehicle. Bouvier is, even by Haitian standards, a remarkably poor community. So why does it exist? Simply because it is home, and for generations it has been home, to hundreds of people who live spread out across the mountain.

And so, early Monday morning, three of us from the Journey, accompanied by six Haitians, left Carrefour and began what would be a nine-hour trek. We at Impact Nations had raised money to purchase school desks. While it was still dark, a group of children from Bouvier excitedly ran down the mountain for three hours to meet us. I was amazed to see them arrive at our starting point, then with only a couple minutes rest, turn around and head up to Bouvier again—this time carrying the school desk materials on their heads and in their arms.

My friend Reg had explained to me that this would be a very strenuous hike. We would have to cross three small rivers and climb three mountains. The trail was treacherous in places, and very steep; in fact, it was too steep for any kind of vehicle, or even horses. Only mules could make the climb. (My wife thought I was being mule-headed to make this climb, so I suppose there was something ironic in Reg's comment.) The trek began with walking knee-deep up the middle of a river for about a mile—so much for keeping my shoes dry! Then we began to climb the first mountain. After an hour or two, we stopped at the last settlement we would see before the mountains. As we rested, Reg asked me one more time if I was sure I was up to this; if not, he wouldn't mind taking me back down. I assured him that I was doing fine.

For nine hours we climbed; it was, without a doubt, the longest, steepest hike of my life. Many times my feet slipped on the loose sand and gravel; every time, before I could fall, a strong arm reached out to steady me. At several places the trail hugged precipices that were hundreds of feet high. Again and again, we would come around a bend on the trail, only to be confronted by spectacular views. About seven hours into the hike, after crossing the third river, we took our final rest stop.

While sitting there, Reg pointed out a spot a few yards away and told me an incredible story. A year earlier, he had taken a group of people from his church up to Bouvier. Among the team was a somewhat older woman. While they were resting at this same place, the woman had suffered a heart attack. After a few moments her heart stopped beating. They tried everything they knew to do, but they could not revive her. They were unsure what to do next; it was further back to the city than to Bouvier, but this last mountain was by far the steepest. They couldn't leave her body there, so one of the men, Celeste, said he would pick her up and carry her to Bouvier. And that is exactly what he did. It took him several hours, but he made it. (I kept thinking about that as I climbed the final two hours; it was the hardest part of the whole trek.) When the team got to the top, Celeste put the woman's dead body down on the ground. Suddenly, the whole team felt a strong presence of the Lord surrounding them. They began to pray that He would bring this woman back to life—even though it had now been close to three hours since her heart had stopped. They prayed several times, and then suddenly, her heart began to beat, she opened her eyes and started to speak. The lady was completely healed. In fact, when they went back down the mountain three days later, she was walking out in front of the whole team!

We arrived at Bouvier just before sunset. Exhausted, we lay down on the floor of the church and quickly fell asleep. For the next two days we toured the area, prayed for the sick, and taught the people about Jesus. I also used this time to scout some possible projects that would help improve life for the community. Before we began the trip to Bouvier, Reg had told me about the unique presence of the Lord that seemed to hang over this tiny community. He was right; at various times I too was aware of the strong presence of the Holy Spirit. On the third day, we walked back to Carrefour; then the next day we flew back to our homes.

When I first arrived at Bouvier, I was unsure why I had felt compelled to make a trip to this isolated community. However, as I reported various accounts about my time there, something interesting happened. Somehow, faith was stirred in a number of those who read the reports and over the following months, a transformation began to take place in Bouvier. A few months later, two men from New York State made the climb up the mountain, bringing with them eight water tanks and the materials needed for water collection systems. One of them was David Pearson, the man who continues to head up our water projects around the world. Now, during the rainy season, many people in Bouvier are able to get their drinking water right in the village and they no longer have to make the long three-and-a-half hour trek.

During the time he was working on installing the tanks at the school, David called and informed me that many of the school children were so hungry, they were in tears. They walked up to *four hours* each way to school, and most of them did it on empty stomachs. When I reported this on our website, someone took up the challenge of sourcing food, while others pledged to cover the costs. A couple of months later, an entire mule train carried over 160,000 dehydrated meals up the mountain. For the first time ever, each child received a daily nutritious meal—enough food was supplied to last for two years.. Others read about the ramshackle school with no windows, no lights and a dirt floor. Over the next six months, two teams—one from Canada and one from Australia—went to Bouvier to build a proper school for over 200 children.

Once again, the Lord was teaching me that I do not, and cannot, know all that He is doing. While I was wondering why I had made this difficult journey, He was carving out a place in my heart for an isolated mountain community, and through that, allowing me to connect with men and women from all over the world whose hearts had been prepared for this exact time and place.

Once again, the Lord was teaching me that I do not, and cannot, know all that He is doing.

This is a lesson that Jesus needs to keep teaching me, over and over again: "We walk by faith, and not by sight."

33

FROM DEATH TO LIFE IN BURUNDI

Burundi is a small country. close to the center of Africa. In 1993, a civil war broke out without warning; over 275,000 people were killed in the ensuing genocide. So, as one would expect, the scars run deeply in this land. One evening, when I was in the city of Bujumbura, I visited with a friend from England who had been living in Burundi for nearly thirty years. Chrissy told me about her life during those terrifying days. She described how the civil war erupted with the sudden outbreak of shooting all around her city. For three weeks, for her to go outside the house was to face the likelihood of dying. She turned out the lights and waited, not knowing exactly what was happening or what the coming days would bring. One night there was a knock on her door. When she opened it, there appeared to be no one there; looking down, she saw a tiny infant lying on the ground. Quickly, she took it inside. For the next couple of days, Chrissy cared for the baby as best she could, feeding the baby milk and whatever other liquids she had. Then a few nights later, there was another knock and another baby was waiting at her doorstep.

This went on for several weeks. When the shooting finally stopped, Chrissy was caring for 35 babies. Although she thought that the parents would eventually return for their children, none ever did.

So her life took a sudden and completely unexpected turn. From that time on, Chrissy has dedicated herself to raising these children. She found a larger facility and others to help her provide the necessary care. In time, the children went to school, first primary, and then secondary. Eventually, some of the children went on to university. And all this time, new children kept coming. As she recounted her story, what impacted me was the tangible sense of family that all these children must have enjoyed. This was not an orphanage; this it was is a home, and Chrissy was their mother. The Lord had provided.

•   •   •

After a few days in Bujumbura, our team headed into the interior to the city of Gitega. With Gitega as our base, we headed out each day to remote villages where we conducted mobile medical clinics, prayed for the sick, and shared the Gospel. We were working in very isolated communities, where some people had never seen a white person. The word spread about the clinics and each morning we were inundated with a lot of very sick people. I remember one morning we got off the bus, and were met by a crowd of over 550 people. More arrived throughout the day. By late morning, there were so many people crowded into the small courtyard in front of the clinic, that three of us led some of the crowd up a hill onto a large field.

First our medical director gave an impromptu lesson on good health practices to the attentive crowd, then I told them about how Jesus loves to heal and invited any who were in pain or sick to raise their hands. Almost all the hands went up. As we started to pray for them, the skies opened. In the ensuing torrential downpour, we assumed that the crowd would scatter; instead, everyone stayed, waiting to receive prayer. The field quickly turned to mud, and still nobody left. In the midst of this drenching, Jesus was healing everyone. After that, my friend RK told the crowd about this Jesus who had healed them and invited them to open their hearts and lives to Christ. RK led the crowd in a prayer. As the rain continued to beat down on us all, *every hand* went up in response to his prayer. But not only that, a great shout arose; many people began to sing and dance in the mud. I had never seen anything like it.

Two days later, we were conducting a medical clinic in another isolated village. A few things from that day also stand out in my memory. Again we encountered incredibly sick people. In fact, the pediatrician on our team set up an infant ICU for forty-eight hours for three babies. The doctor told me that if we hadn't arrived on that particular day and treated these children, they would have not survived. As we have seen happen all over the world, once again the Lord had brought us to exactly the right place, at exactly the right time.

I remember being at the intake table when a tall, distinguished looking woman came to me. When I asked what she needed, she simply opened her colorful African robe partway, and showed me the baby that she had just given birth to at the side of the road. Another one of my clearest memories was of a young man who carried his father to the clinic. The old man's legs were so twisted and deformed that his feet were permanently locked over his shoulders, on either side of his head. In this position, the man could not even sit on the ground, but had to lie on his side. Our team began to pray for him. As they continued praying, his legs began to loosen. Eventually they came down to a normal position. The man could sit in a chair. There was great celebration from the villagers. Then the team turned their attention to his son, a young man in his early twenties. When they asked this young man his name, he replied that he didn't have one—his father and mother had never even given him a name. The team was stunned. After talking and praying with him, they asked if he would like to have a name--when he eagerly said yes, they named him John. I cannot imagine the wounding and rejection a child would feel who had never even been given a name by his parents, yet this son had cared enough for his crippled father to bring him to the clinic.

His father and mother had never even given him a name.

On our final day in Burundi, we drove up into the mountains to a remote Pygmy village. As our bus climbed to over 7,000 feet, the air turned surprisingly cool for so near the equator, and the hills looked like the highlands of Scotland. We were headed to a small village of 360 people. A man named Bosco had asked us to come to this place, where there was only *one* believer. When we arrived, we found they had set up some tarps on the side of the mountain in the middle of a beautiful (and very steep) meadow. It certainly was the most lopsided clinic we ever conducted! The entire village came out to the clinic; many were sick, but others were just curious to see this group of people from across the ocean. While the crowd waited, we took the opportunity to teach them some good health practices. Then my dentist friend, Kenneth, talked to them about taking good care of their teeth. I still remember, when he asked the crowd how many of them had been to a dentist; all we saw were puzzled faces. Then when someone finally asked what was on all of their minds: "What is a dentist?" After a good laugh, Kenneth went ahead and gave them

Then when someone finally asked what was on all of their minds: "What is a dentist?"

some good lessons about oral hygiene. As we had done in the previous village a few days earlier, we then told them about Jesus and how He loves to heal. Once again, the Lord moved in a powerful way; to our knowledge, *everyone* was healed. Then we explained the Gospel and invited them to give their lives to Jesus. Every hand went up. Once again, a great shout of joy arose. All day, whether in the clinic, in people's huts, or out on the field, everyone gave their lives to Christ. Bosco was almost beside himself with joy; he announced that from that day forward, he would give himself to caring for these new believers. What was happening in that village was so remarkable that I telephoned a radio station in London, England that I had been working with for some time. I did a live report right then and there about this remarkable move of God. The news went out all over Great Britain that very hour.

Hours later, I lay in my bed, too excited to sleep. It felt like there was electricity pulsing through my body. For the first time in my life, I had seen an entire community come to Jesus in a single day. When I thought of Chrissy's story, I realized once again that the power of the resurrection is always at work, rescuing, renewing and restoring men, women, children, villages and even entire nations.

34

MULTIPLIED IN THE GIVING

I think the first time it happened (at least that I was aware of) was in a neighborhood church that met in a community center in a poor part of our city. There is no doubt about what happened because I can count past 72. I suppose I should explain.

We had planned a 'love feast' for our small congregation. It was to be a meal for about 70 of us. I had prepared some activities around sharing communion at tables. I had something new in mind, something that I thought would both celebrate and encourage the intimacy that had developed among us. Definitely, this was an 'us' time.

There was only one problem; a few of the group hadn't got the memo. They thought that this was an outreach, a meal for the poor in our community. Without me being aware, the word had spread quickly. So as our love feast was about to begin, the neighborhood started to arrive. We set up an extra table, then another one, and another one...Before long, worried church members started quietly suggesting that we take up a quick collection and head to the nearest grocery store. My mood was getting worse by the minute. After all, this was supposed to be our intimate church family time; everything was going wrong. My wife said to each concerned person, "Let's just see what the Lord has in mind. We'll feed the community first and then the rest of us will eat what's left over."

Here is where the counting to 72 comes in. That is how many barbequed pork buns had been prepared. (We counted them twice, just to make sure.) Among the other food that was laid out was a really big bowl of fruit salad. We prayed for the food and invited our neighborhood guests to serve themselves first. I watched with concern as they piled the pork buns on their plates—two, three, even four high. (I'm not exaggerating.) I remember heading out of the dining area just to walk off some of my frustration. When I came back in, all of the neighbors were eating and most of our congregation as well. I looked at the fruit salad bowl and was surprised, as it appeared that no one had taken any—the bowl was still almost full. Then I looked at the trays of pork buns. It was only then that I realized that something very out-of-the-ordinary was happening. You guessed it. There were still lots of buns left even though we had a large crowd and everyone was enjoying eating their fill.

A few minutes later, after many people went back for seconds, my wife and I were the last to eat. We both had full plates, including fruit salad and pork buns. Interestingly though, after we finished helping ourselves, no fruit salad or barbequed pork buns were left. Hmm.

The atmosphere was suddenly very festive. My carefully

planned love feast was blown apart. No communion at the table, no well-organized activities. Instead, there was laughter, singing (both Christian and secular songs), and the room was filled with the sound of new friendships. One of our congregation got up and talked about how much Jesus loved what was happening. Several of our guests gave their lives to Him that night.

Since then, I've watched Jesus sneak up on us on numerous occasions and surprise everyone by multiplying what we have. In one of the biggest garbage dumps in Asia, He took the 550 lunches that we had prepared for poor and hungry children, and turned them into 800—because that is how many kids showed up when the word got out that there was food available. And you know what? Once

> *He took the 550 lunches that we had prepared for poor and hungry children, and turned them into 800.*

again, the last kid in line got the last lunch. Then there was the time in a town in Uganda, when we had prepared anti-parasite medicine for 150 people (like the buns, we counted beforehand). Almost 400 people showed up. Instead of sending them away or deciding that it would be unfair to just give medicine to some people, we decided to hand out the medicine until it ran out. You can guess the rest of the story. That's right—every person received the much-needed anti-parasite medicine.

I don't know how He does it. I never *saw* buns or fruit salad or lunches or medicine multiply; it just did. Maybe that's how it was for the disciples when they started handing out the bread and fish to the hungry crowd. Nobody saw how it happened, but the *how* didn't matter. What mattered was that they stepped out, in spite of the obvious lack.

What matters is that I step out, even when I don't have enough—enough compassion, faith, patience or time. Because in the economy of the Kingdom, multiplication happens in the act of giving in spite of my weakness or lack. After all, Jesus promised to take the tiny mustard seed that we give Him, and turn it into a tree—or a few more barbecued pork buns.

35

BREAKTHROUGH IN NORTHERN INDIA

More than forty times I have had the joy of leading teams from around the world on frontline ministry excursions to 15 different developing nations. We have gone to remote villages and crowded slums, to prisons and massive garbage dumps. We have traveled to countries in Africa, Southeast Asia, the Caribbean, Central America and South America. And everywhere we have gone, without exception, Jesus has moved in our midst in great power and compassion. Recently I was reading over my journal entries from one of these trips, our first Journey of Compassion to the Punjab in northern India. Here are some excerpts:

Our first day out in the village was remarkable. We were in a village where no house churches had yet been established, and our ministry partner, Randeep, did not know how we would be received. We were instructed to offer to pray but not be insistent in any way, as we did not want to offend the people. When we approached the people waiting in the courtyard for medical attention and asked if we could pray, immediately they would say 'yes'. From the very first person, the healings began. Our team prayed nonstop for hours. Almost everyone was healed. Many came to Jesus in this Sikh and Hindu village. A woman who was paralyzed down one side of her body was carried into the courtyard; she was completely healed and walked out with great joy. Deaf ears opened. Blind eyes received sight. And always, people were giving their hearts to Jesus. The people were literally pulling on the shirts of the team, asking for prayer -- it was almost overwhelming. I saw team members with tears of joy at what the Lord was doing. Meanwhile, we provided medical care for almost 200 people.

The people were literally pulling on the shirts of the team, asking for prayer.

We returned to the hotel for an hour's rest, before coming back to the village for the first outreach. The band was playing in a large courtyard when we arrived. The courtyard was packed to overflowing and many more stood on surrounding roofs; people even began to climb a high wall (about 14 feet) in order to see. Team members shared powerful healing testimonies from the day; afterwards, I preached about how the Kingdom had come to their village today. I invited the crowd to give their lives to Jesus, then led them in a prayer. I asked those who had prayed this prayer for the first time to raise their hands. I think that *every hand went up. Every* hand.

An hour later, when we were eating, Randeep told me that they already had eight 'houses of peace'—by which he meant that already eight families had asked if their homes could host a house church. We are all so amazed that the Lord had done so much in one day. (Before our five days in the Punjab were over, 50 families would ask to host a house church!)

As I finish this journal entry, we are getting ready to leave for our second village. Come Lord Jesus, come.

•   •   •

Another journal entry:

I have been to India seventeen times, but this time we are seeing something that I have never witnessed before. Instead of suspicion or hesitation, the Gospel is being embraced by almost everyone. I say 'almost', because there must have been some people who did not come forward to give their lives to Jesus, but I didn't see any of them. Once again in this next village, every hand went up. There was a huge crush of people who immediately came forward in response to the invitation. The crowd at the front was so dense that many of the Impact team had to go to the back in order to have room to pray for people. And once again, healing after healing took place. Some members reported every person they prayed for was healed. One thing that has impacted me greatly over the past two days, is the eagerness with which the older Sikh gentlemen respond. This is something I have not seen before in the Sikh culture.

There were so many healings throughout the day—both during the medical clinic and at the outdoor meeting in the evening—that I will only mention a few highlights. Merve, who is heading up the medical team for this Journey, had an older woman come to the clinic. She was deaf, so Merve looked at her ears with his scope. Both of her eardrums were 'atrophied' (his term); they were opaque and shriveled. Merve prayed for her and suddenly she could hear perfectly. Amazed, he looked in her ears again with the scope. Merve now saw two soft, translucent eardrums that he told me were like those of a baby. Later a man with severe cataracts came to him. After prayer, the man could see perfectly. Merve looked at his eyes with his instrument and the cataracts had completely disappeared.

Tina prayed for a woman who received healing then gave her life to Jesus. A few minutes later she came back with six more women. Tina prayed for each one of them in turn; each one was healed and each one asked Jesus into her life. I prayed for a man with thick glasses who had trouble seeing objects in the distance. After praying three times, there was no difference. Then I remembered that Stephen had been used in that morning in the healing of a couple of people's vision, so I asked him to come over and pray. Stephen prayed for about 5 seconds and the young man's eyes were completely restored. (A couple of hours later, I saw the man walking in the village—without his glasses.)

The leaders of this village of about 2,500 came to Randeep and told him that we were the first group of 'white people' to ever come to serve in their village. Once again we are reminded that the cornerstone of the Gospel is to demonstrate the love of God, both practically and supernaturally. Follow-up has already begun with Randeep's *team. They have identified 'houses of peace' (Luke 10:6) where new house churches will be started right away. The early fruit from India and Impact Nations working together with Randeep's network has been wonderful.*

• • •

Following three days of medical clinics and outdoor meetings, we went into the streets of two of the villages with water filters and prayer teams. Everywhere we went we met people eager to hear about Jesus—and then to open their lives to him. One distinguished Sikh gentleman approached a team member and said: "I want Jesus now!" As we would begin to pray for a person in need, immediately a whole group would congregate asking for prayer. Entire families were being led to the Lord. People gathered their friends and brought them to us so that they too could hear the Gospel. Everywhere people were asking Randeep if his team would come again to their homes. There are now eighteen 'houses of peace' waiting to host new house churches in three villages.

One distinguished Sikh gentleman approached a team member and said: "I want Jesus now!"

• • •

One morning I received two phone calls: the first one from Dr. Victor Choudhrie, the founder of this amazing house church movement. He had heard about what the Lord was doing in the Punjab and he phoned, wanting to hear about it directly from me. Then my friend Anuroop called, because he, too, had heard. As I shared our delight with the way in which so many people received Christ, Anuroop said this to me: "Steve, do you realize that all over this nation believers have said for a long time that the Punjab is the hardest area in India to receive the Gospel? Now that has changed."

God put a hunger in my heart for the Punjab to turn to Christ when I first visited it 16 years ago. What a privilege and joy to see this desire beginning to be fulfilled.

You have a saying, 'Four more months till harvest.'
But I tell you, open your eyes and look at the
fields ready for harvest now. (John 4:35)

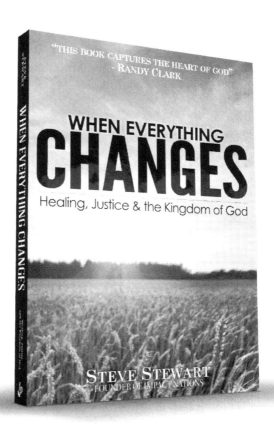

If you have enjoyed these stories, you can read more in:

WHEN EVERYTHING CHANGES:
Healing, Justice and the Kingdom of God

If you would like to find out more about the ministry of
Impact Nations, or would like to come on a Journey of
Compassion, please go to: www.impactnations.org

ACKNOWLEDGEMENTS

No book is completed without the help, correction and encouragement of many people. *The Journey* is no exception. In many ways it is the product of numerous lives intersecting over many years. I am so thankful for all those who have enriched my life in so many ways.

I want to especially thank Jenny, Karen, and Don for all the hours of reading, re-reading, and editing. Thank you, Jenny for your encouragement in the early days of this book. Thanks, Karen for your creative ideas and reading of each draft. Thank you, Don for both your willingness and ability to go over each story in minute detail.

Thanks Ben, for all your work to format and lay out the final version. God has gifted you in many ways.

Thank you, Christina for so often being a sounding board as I tried to determine whether or not to include material in this book. As always, thank you for your encouragement.

Much of this book has come out of my work with Impact Nations. I am very grateful for the steadfast support of so many people—

- Our overseas partners who work in the trenches day after day, developing and supervising transformational projects, leading people to Jesus, and making disciples. You are amazing.

- The Impact Nations board members. Thanks for all the years of walking with Christina and me.
- The hundreds of people who sacrificed their time, energy and finances to travel to nations on the other side of the world in order to participate in advancing God's Kingdom. You truly are rescuing lives and transforming communities.

Most of all, thank You, Jesus for inviting me to the dance.